JOYCE LANDORF
OFFERS ENCOURAGEMENT IN TIMES
OF DIFFICULTY
AND ASSURANCE IN TIMES OF PEACE:

ON GROWING THROUGH SUFFERING: "I am firmly convinced that Paul's words, likening us to God's garden, are true, especially when he writes: 'In this work, we work with God, and that means you are a field under God's cultivation.' (1 Cor. 3:9, Phillips).

"If it's true that we are a garden or a field cultivated by God, I am sure one of the best garden tools the Lord uses in our lives to produce fruit and stimulate growth is the digging trowel of suffering."

ON GROWING THROUGH PAIN: "We suffer pain and hurt as God allows it, but we never suffer needlessly. No! Our suffering prepares us as nothing else can to identify and recognize pain in others and to comfort with wisdom and tenderness."

THE HIGH COST OF GROWING
by Joyce Landorf

Author of *His Stubborn Love, Let's Have a Banquet* and *The Richest Lady in Town*

ABOUT THE AUTHOR

JOYCE LANDORF is a bestselling author whose books reflect her various identities as successful vocalist, public speaker, journalist, wife, mother and grandmother. She has written twelve previous books including *The Richest Lady in Town*. She lives with her family in Hacienda Heights, California.

THE HIGH
COST
OF
GROWING

Joyce Landorf

BANTAM BOOKS
Toronto • New York • London • Sydney

THE HIGH COST OF GROWING

*A Bantam Book / published by arrangement with
Thomas Nelson Inc., Publishers*

PRINTING HISTORY

Thomas Nelson edition published April 1978

Bantam edition / March 1979

1st printing ... February 1979	3rd printing ..... May 1982
2nd printing .... March 1980	4th printing .. November 1982
	5th printing ... March 1984

*Scripture quotations marked TLB are taken from The Living
Bible (Wheaton, Ill.: Tyndale House Publishers, 1971) and are
used by permission.*

*Scripture quotations marked RSV are from the Revised Stan-
dard Version of the Bible, copyright 1946, 1952, © 1971, 1973
by the Division of Christian Education of the National Council
of the Churches of Christ of the U.S.A. and are used by permission.*

*Scripture quotations marked "Phillips" are from J. B. Phillips:
The New Testament in Modern English. Revised Edition ©
1958, 1960, 1972. Used by permission of the Macmillan Company and by William Collins, Sons & Co., Ltd., London and
Glasgow.*

*Bantam Books are published by Bantam Books, Inc. Its trade-
mark, consisting of the words "Bantam Books" and the por-
trayal of a rooster, is Registered in U.S. Patent and Trademark
Office and in other countries. Marca Registrada. Bantam
Books, Inc., 666 Fifth Avenue, New York, New York 10103.*

PRINTED IN THE UNITED STATES OF AMERICA

H   14 13 12 11 10 9 8 7 6 5

My continued thanks to two gifted gals
Brenda Arnold
and
Sheila Rapp
for their typing, editing, and especially
their spelling!

My special thanks to Pete Gillquist, who by
asking the right questions began this book.

Contents

Chapter One

The High Cost
of Growing

There is an old nursery rhyme that goes,

> Mary, Mary, quite contrary,
> How does your garden grow?

The improbable answer is,

> With silver bells, and cockle shells,
> And pretty maids all in a row.

We smile at the whimsical verse, for we know too well what makes a garden grow, and it has little to do with shells, bells, or statue-like maids lined up in a row.

What farmer, after all, expects his fields to yield a harvest merely by his looking through a seed catalog, choosing his crops, and then settling back in his rocking chair to wait? If he thinks his garden and fields will grow without his cultivating the ground, planting the seed, weeding, fertilizing, watering, and harvesting, he's more off his rocker than on.

Yet in the same improbable, fairy-tale way, I find we often think Christians grow more like Christ every day without any action, any suffering, doubts, or pain. It is rather as if we have a little set of doodads here, a bit of mumbo-jumbo there; and a few cockle shells and silver bells later we arrive at full-blown Christianhood. It's as if we become instantly sensitive to both the Holy Spirit and others; then magically we develop into

1

giants of the faith with nothing happening in between. No fuss, no muss, and certainly no hassle.

Not so!

The hard, cold labors of farming are what produce the crops and rich harvests, and it is just so with our spiritual growth. Growing by pain, stress, doubts, obedience, differences, and past and present situations is what the Christian life is all about. Visible growth is the best thermometer in the world by which to take our spiritual temperatures. It can tell us whether we are alive in Christ or not.

Over twenty years ago I awakened to a new life in Jesus Christ. What I did not know then but know now is that coming to Christ was the event, but **staying** alive in Him is a life-long process.

Not too long after I accepted the Lord I was filled and bubbling over with an enthusiastic desire to tell the whole world about the gospel. I was convinced that since I could sing He would use that talent, and I'd be everywhere singing for His glory.

However, no one asked me to sing and no doors opened, so I questioned the Lord as to how He wanted me to give the gospel to the world.

"Be a wife first, a mother to Rick and Laurie second, and later I'll take care of these other things," came the Lord's quick, matter-of-fact answer. It wasn't **exactly** what I'd had in mind.

I accepted the Lord's "no" and followed His direction, not because I was the marvelously obedient sainted Joyce, but rather because when I examined the alternatives of living outside God's will it scared me to death!

Have you ever pestered, begged, or nagged God with some request, had Him answer no and then days, months, or even years later breathed a sigh of relief at the wisdom of that "no"? I have. In fact, when I think about that first no of the Lord's, I can see Him in my mind's eye, shaking His head, smiling, and I can hear Him saying,

"You see Joyce, I've always known what's best for

you. I gave you a "no" answer not because I didn't love you, didn't think you capable or talented enough, or didn't need you to share the good news, but because **you** needed a time to grow."

I know now the Lord wanted me to have twenty years of growing before I wrote a line about it, much less a book! I needed those twenty years. I still need the growing process, and I will have that need to grow until I see Him face to face.

Growing is that intangible moving force that stretches our minds and souls in a thousand directions at once. Yet, why then is there so much misunderstanding, passivity, and just plain fantasizing over growth? And why isn't there an overwhelming desire on our part, as Christians, to grow up?

The reason is simply that growing is something none of us considers our favorite love-to-do thing. Generally speaking, it is no thrill to grow. As I recall there was no glamour and no excitement associated in my mind with being wife and mother as there seemed to be in singing for God.

I suppose it has to do with the fact that growing is an action verb. It requires a decision of the will, a commitment to do, or at the very least some kind of change. Most of us loathe moving out of our comfortable ruts and rocking chairs. Yet, growing up in Christ means just that—moving and changing.

Haven't you wondered from time to time why some Christians are so extra special? They add joy to your life even if your eyes only meet in a fleeting glance across a crowded room; or one smile and handshake opens the flow of conversation as if you had been friends for ages. Growing Christians increase your perspective, enlarge your capacity for learning, and leave you filled up beyond measure.

Other Christians drain your supply source, taking so much spiritual energy away from you that when you leave them you are exhausted. Sometimes not even your sense of humor is intact.

As I have observed and talked with hundreds—no, make that thousands—of Christians, the ones who are dynamic and loving people are constantly blossoming, growing, and bearing fruit in Christ. They are not the "arrivers," as Keith Miller would say, but the "becomers."

I have made a list of people whom I believe are **growing** in one way or another. Some of them are not Christians, and so they do not add to my spiritual insight or depth; but they do have a great deal to teach me about growing. My list is entitled "I sometimes wish I were _____ ."

Now, before you think I'm unhappy being me, let me hasten to say, God has made me Joyce Landorf. He has made only one of me and while on some days, I am not too pleased with me, I know I am loved, forgiven—and not only accepted by God, but **chosen**. But the people on my list possess qualities I admire and would like to emulate. As you review the list, I hope you will begin to understand, as I have, the conditions for growth.

I sometimes wish I were . . .

Barbra Streisand. She is a musician's musician who tells her vocal chords to do this and that and this again without losing control, pitch, or beat. And her voice flawlessly obeys.

Martene Craig. She can conduct any group, choir, orchestra, or collection of people set before her without a single qualm. She can also go from the farthest out rock music to the heaviest Bach or Beethoven number without any trace of musical or cultural shock.

Dinah Shore. She comes across on television as an easy-come, easy-go, relaxed lady. She asks all the right questions and interviews guests with apparently little or no fuss.

Chris Evert. She hits that little white ball over the net with an effortless flick of her wrist.

John Naber. He slices through water with the speed and grace of a dolphin.

Clare Bauer. Beautiful and brainy—inside and out.

4

Dale Evans. The older she gets, the more she glows.

Corrie ten Boom. Same thing! She glows even though she's had eighty-four years of glowing.

Dick Landorf. He is a banker with everything under control and he never gets lost in the process. He also is the most tough and tender man alive.

Dr. James Dobson. He is a psychology expert.

Dr. Leonard Buchanan. He is an engineering expert.

Dr. Edward B. Cole and **Dr. Keith Korstjens.** They are theology experts.

Dr. James White. He is a surgeon and medical expert.

I could go on, but I'm sure you already have enough to work with. The real point of giving you this list is to show you that the people on it have learned two important truths: (1) what we become is **not** the result of merely possessing a God-given talent, and (2) the high cost of growing must be paid if improvement and eventual excellence are desired.

Saint Peter is quite clear about our talents when he says, "God has given each of you some special abilities . . ." (1 Pet. 4:10, TLB).

We all have special gifts, talents, or physical abilities, but the key to real success lies in what we choose to do with them.

For instance,

Barbra was born with that four-octave voice. But developing it, perfecting it, and learning to read music was done in practice rooms and with great expense of time and energy.

Martene has loved music all her life, but it was the hard work and study, not the love, that changed her into the fantastic minister of music she is today.

Dinah, although she comes on television looking relaxed and full of ad-libs, has given serious and careful attention to the biographical material on each guest. In other words she has done her homework and has done it well.

Chris would have stayed on the tennis court in someone's backyard, impressing a handful of family and neighborhood friends, except for the hours of exhausting, determined workouts.

John would have cut a dashing figure at the beach or pool, but he would have never been awarded his Olympic gold medal for his good looks alone.

Clare has never settled for mediocrity in **anything,** so she is always striving for perfection in whatever task is before her.

Dale's newest book, **Trials, Tears and Triumph,** is a study of how God has caused her to grow. For my money she has every right to be an ugly, embittered lady. Yet her incredible losses have been the power behind her glow.

Corrie's glow did not come suddenly. It was not a quick happening, like turning on a light bulb, that ushered her into bright sainthood. No, she grew, expanded, and began her glow in the horrors of the Ravensbruck concentration camp under Hitler's dictatorship.

Dick's tough and tender ways have used up the better part of twenty years. My husband is constantly **becoming** God's man. I can see God's hand on the loom of Dick's life—weaving and working a man of sturdy cloth.

And of course the various doctorates of my friends were not generously bestowed as honorary degrees, but in each case the doctorate was hard earned and obtained at great physical and mental expense.

All of these people, plus many others I have met and talked with, have not been automatically sensational, successful, or obviously super-spiritual. In each case, while there was initial talent, there was an exacting toll paid for growth and development, and there always will be. Maturing and growing, whether it is mentally, physically, or spiritually, are always with difficult.

I suspect many of you agree with that last statement. Even back in high school and college, which of us did not want to cut class, skip school, or play hooky at least once during the semester?

For our own individual reasons we didn't seem to

want to learn any more arithmetic equations, and more spelling words, or any more grammatically correct phrases. And yet growing and learning meant we had to concentrate, study, and work our brains overtime. It would have been a lot easier to duck out of school. And so it is—whether we are talking about the formal academic institutions or the big, real school of life.

So how does a Christian really grow?

1. Growing is a very slow process that extends over our entire lifetime.

We live in a world of instant replays. Add water and stir. We are impressed with speed, and so to develop slowly and by God's timing in the midst of our culture is probably one of the most difficult lessons to learn.

We want instant sainthood. We want to immediately find the right words to comfort the bereaving family and friends. We pray for on-the-spot success and spout on-the-spot solutions. We want total recall of the appropriate Scripture verses. And worse than any of these, we glibly quote, "Be patient with me for God isn't through with me yet," but don't mean it for one single second. We are the most impatient people in the world, particularly when it comes to our own development. I have talked with many defeated Christians who say, "I just don't understand God's timing in this." What they really mean is "What's taking so long?" and "Why doesn't God hurry up?"

So the first principle of becoming a growing, expanding Christian is to understand that maturing is a slow, never-ending process. It goes on and on. Sometimes growth is like a child's game—we take three giant steps forward and then are made to take one backward. That in itself is enough to confuse and discourage us. Yet growth does not come in a highly regimented fashion. We don't take it three times a day like our morning, noon, and bedtime doses of medicine. It comes in spurts, and usually at a time when we least expect it.

Only God knows how much growing we can assimilate into our systems during one given period of time.

7

So be patient with the Lord and trust His timing. He really is in control, and believe it or not, He knows what He is doing.

In addition to growing covering a long period of time, there is a second factor we must understand about God's process.

2. **Christians often grow and mature best in the heavy, cold darkness of stress, pain, various anxieties, fear, and by all kinds of emotional, physical, and mental suffering.**

The title of Margaret Clarkson's book **Grace Grows Best in Winter** is not only poetic and beautiful, but terribly true.

While it is possible to learn and mature as a Christian during the bright, fair-weather times of our lives, the rate of spiritual development is greatly diminished compared to the rate during the storms of life. Many of us know that when tragedy slams into us with the force of a tornado, or when stress and pain pull all the rugs out from under our feet, the chances of our growing are greatly accelerated and greatly enhanced if we are careful to see them.

I can hear someone saying out there, "Oh, Joyce, God is not a cruel God, inflicting these terrible things on us for our benefit. He does not want us to suffer, to be sick, or to be in pain. In fact, there are many ways to grow in Christ other than through heartaches and stress." Still another person says, "Why, I know for a fact God teaches us to grow through daily devotions, Bible study, discipling groups, and a dedicated prayer life."

To all of this I can say a hearty "Amen!" We do not have a cruel God who gets some weird kick out of seeing us squirm under pressure. And yes, we do grow from good, positive experiences. In fact, I will deal with some of them in a later chapter. But the point is that Christians grow **best** and experience greater results under God-allowed crises and problems.

To some people this concept of God using suffering, stress, and pain to bring forth growth is an intolerable thought. Truly it is one of the most misunderstood and mistaught teachings of our day. Yet it remains firm: the Lord uses all of the hard, cold, difficult things of this world to bring about development and growth. We need to be reminded that He used suffering, adverse situations, and disappointing circumstances in the lives of people mentioned throughout the Bible, and some of them were people who were far more spiritually advanced than any of us. So why do we have such a hard time with the continual problems of suffering?

Basically, we don't want to pay the high cost of growing, which may mean stress or suffering losses. And secondly, to us these avenues of growth and maturity rarely make sense.

When a young piano student is flailing away at Hanon or Czerny exercises several hours a day, it is very difficult for him to make a great deal of sense out of it. Yet those repetitious trips up and down the keyboard, and the aching muscles that follow, all make a great deal of sense a few years later when he sits down to play a flawlessly executed piano concert.

How easy it is to look admiringly at others, to compare our successes with theirs, or to wish that we could achieve the same level of excellence, and all the while ignore what God wants us to do with our own lives.

There are many other ways to grow and none of them are easy. Growth is expensive, but I encourage you to look not only at the price of growing but also at the rich harvest God has in mind for you to reap.

Chapter Two

Growing Through Suffering

We are never ripe till we have
been made so by suffering.

—Henry Ward Beecher

Pete Gillquist, author and recently turned publishing editor, sat before me. His long, lanky frame covered
one end of my couch as he talked.

"Joyce," he said in a quiet probing voice, "you are
not just churning out these books one after another like
some factory assembly line machine. I've read them,
and with each book I find progress and real growth.
Something is responsible for the growth in your life."

And then, even more directly and deliberately, he
leaned forward and asked, "Tell me, how **do** you
grow?"

My reaction was instantly twofold: pleased, yet surprised. I was pleased because suddenly I was a little
hazel-eyed, blond-haired girl again. It was as if Pete
had taken me over to the measuring marks my mother
used to make on the wall, patted my head, and pro-
nounced, "Wow. Look at that! You're two inches taller
than the last pencil mark."

Since I have always contended that the Christian life
should be a never-ending growing process, it was
beautiful to hear my progress being confirmed and to
learn that the signs of maturity were showing—at least
according to Pete's spiritual yardstick.

But secondly, I was surprised because at no other

time during my twenty years as a Christian has anyone ever pointedly asked about my growth in the Lord.

Then a depressing thought surfaced and skipped across my mind. Oh dear, did no one ask because no one could see any evidence of growth? I remembered that marvelous yet disturbing song Dave Boyer sings which in part says, "If you were arrested for being a Christian, would there be enough evidence to convict you?" and for a few moments it gave me quite a bad time. Mentally I moved on.

What an intriguing question—"How do you grow?"

How does anyone grow? Do all Christians mature and develop in specific and identical manners, or do we grow like children—in spurts, with different speeds and intensities? Does God use varied methods and vastly different timetables for us?

Most of all, my conscience pricked me as I sat before Pete because I thought about all the times I have been in the presence of a real, live, growing-before-my-eyes person and failed to ask him or her about their secret ways of growing. It was a depressing thought because I had missed the moment and not taken advantage of the opportunity. I had lost encounters that had been pregnant with learning.

After a few seconds of stunned silence, I came face up to the answer about my own personal growing.

"Pete, if there is evidence of growth in my life—and I fervently pray there is—then it is due to two kinds of suffering."

"Suffering?" Pete tilted his head and looked quizzically at me, and I realized my statement must have sounded vaguely pious, if not downright stilted and stuffy.

I tried to explain.

"Yes, suffering—the **emotional** suffering of my childhood and young adult life long ago, and the more recent **physical** suffering of my life now."

All he said was, "Tell me about it."

Then for the better part of two hours I spoke with him about the two types of suffering that have consistently and inevitably produced and contributed to my spiritual growth.

Recalling the hurts and disappointments that afternoon to Pete was very difficult for me to do and quite painful. Reviving our past in objective honesty usually is.

Much of what I said had to be brought up out of some pretty deep caves within me, and my confrontation with truth was an unsettling yet marvelously healing time. I will never regret or forget the afternoon. But then, growing is always like that—a difficult yet unforgettable experience.

I am firmly convinced that Paul's words, likening us to God's garden, are true, especially when he writes: "In this work, we work with God, and that means that you are a field under God's cultivation . . ." (1 Cor. 3:9, Phillips).

It was Charles Spurgeon, one of history's great ministers of God, who said:

> Oh, to have one's soul as a field under heavenly cultivation, no wilderness but a garden of the Lord, walled around by grace, planted by instruction, visited by love, weeded by heavenly discipline, guarded by divine power. One's soul thus favored is prepared to yield fruit unto the glory of God.

If it is true that we are a garden or a field cultivated by God, I am sure one of the best garden tools the Lord uses in our lives to produce fruit and stimulate growth is the digging trowel of suffering.

How hard it is to let Him dig. Every time He uses suffering to cultivate and aerate the soil around us, we are sure our lives are being uprooted and bound for annihilation.

Yet, quite the opposite is true. God uses his trowels, tractors, and plows with utmost discretion and wisdom, and all that digging produces healthy, growing people.

There are many kinds of human suffering and, of course, the most obvious and "seeable" kind is the physical. For example, the physical pain of a debilitating disease, the chronic pain of a bone or muscle problem, or the wearisome pain of a dysfunction somewhere in our anatomy all produce a wild, ancient kind of suffering.

There is also a suffering that is easily concealed and sometimes hard to identify, but the pain is just as real as the physical suffering. It is the emotional and mental suffering of our inner being. Let's consider further this kind of pain.

Many of us spend a goodly portion of our lives either disguising this pain, ignoring it, or shoving it way down into our subconscious. Some of us manage to forget it altogether, and it lies inside us, locked away out of our view. Nevertheless, this emotional and mental suffering is just as corrosive, wild, and ancient.

Chronologically, the first suffering we generally run into is the emotional suffering of our childhood that often causes the traumas of our early adult years.

I shall not bore you with the specifics and neverending parade of hurts and disappointments of my own childhood. My early life had its share of positive approval, especially from my mother, but it also had many negative and disappointing factors. I have not revealed those negative factors in past books nor do I intend to start now. And besides, I have a better reason for not sharing the details of my childhood with you. I am wise enough and old enough to know that your painful childhood stories and experiences may very well top mine.

But mark this down somewhere permanently: **each of us has indeed suffered.** For some it has been to a minor degree. For others the suffering they experienced during childhood has left wounds which are almost irreparable and which, to this day, still fester quietly within them.

Once or twice, here and there, I have met individuals who seemingly have escaped the hassles of traumatic emotional suffering during their childhoods, but it's not too often.

Our own two children are interesting examples. When our twenty-four-year-old son Rick and daughter-in-love Teresa were playing the communications game "Tell It Like It Is," Rick drew a card that read, "Complete the statement, 'One thing I missed during my childhood was . . .'"

Teresa told me that Rick looked at her and in a "I'm-shocked-you'd-even-ask" tone of voice replied, "Nothing! I missed nothing during my childhood!"

His statement warmed my heart. However, I suspect if we picked and probed long enough and deeply enough, we could come up with a few things Rick might have missed or at least wishes had been different.

However, I am positive our twenty-two-year-old daughter Laurie, who was born with a hearing loss in both ears, would have answered the question in a vastly different way. I need not ask her to know that what she "missed" during her childhood was the taken-for-granted privilege of hearing the soft, quiet sounds of the world around her.

I have often wondered how the specific childhood sufferings of the great giants in the Bible affected their adult lives.

Did David the psalmist ever look back on his lonely life as a shepherd boy and long for it to have been different? Did he ever fantasize about a good relationship with his brothers as opposed to the one he had? Was his later friendship with Jonathan forged out of his family's rejection and lack of approval? I imagine so, and I highly doubt that anyone in David's family fully understood the great poetic, talented genius that tended the family's sheep herds and took lunches to the brothers in battle. Even when young David was anointed king, I doubt that anyone in his immediate family was too overwhelmed by the honor or glory of it.

In any case, we are all products of our childhood experiences. Our adult performance and behavior is programmed like a computer, for better or worse, in our early years.

If it were possible to clearly label people according

to their childhood experiences and categorize them into neat little boxes, I think we would need,

• A small box for the low percentage of people who had few or no negative hassles and who have experienced a relatively trouble-free childhood.

• A rather large box for the majority of people who have had a mixture of both positive and negative factors and who have experienced a sometimes insecure and unbalanced, yet fairly routine, childhood.

• A medium-sized box for the people who have had more troubling, negative factors than positive and who are still trying to cope with them today.

• A small box for the low percentage of people who never had one single positive influence in their lives and whose childhood produced a torrent of violent and tragic factors from which they may never recover.

When I see those boxes in my head and examine the stories that come out of all of them, I am made aware of a slightly sticky problem, and with reluctance I write about it.

There seems to be a traditional tendency among Christian parents and families to believe that their children, by a magical act of God, will escape all the emotional hurts and bruises of childhood—that they will automatically be in the first box and have a pain-free childhood. It is as if being a church-going, born-again family were a guaranteed security blanket that would protect and insulate each member of the family from any harm.

I can say that statistically the divorce rate, juvenile crime rate, cases of drug abuse, child abuse, incest, homosexuality, and alcoholism (and I could go on) are **definitely lower** in born-again families. Nevertheless, these tragic, horrendous things do happen and are happening in the Christian home of today. Every contemporary Christian counselor, psychologist, and minister has seen the wide path of evidence sin is making in the meadows of Christian lives.

To our sad horror, we have known the Bible teacher who is a child-abuse mother; the chairman of the board of deacons who practices incest with his four daughters; the minister of music who leads a double life as a heterosexual and homosexual; the Christian graduate of a Christian college who has turned to drugs and alcohol because her stepfather sexually molested and raped her from the time she was four years old until she ran away from home at sixteen; the once enthusiastic missionary who has returned and is convinced she is absolutely worthless and who now rots in total depression in a back bedroom of her house; or the pastor's wife who has venereal disease because of her husband's affairs. Shocking? Yes, but sadly true.

These people all **exist** within the church. To believe things like this are not happening in the Christian home is an attractive but foolish and highly erroneous philosophy. Scores of ministers, Christian counselors and psychologists, and dedicated laymen and women are unfortunately in the position to verify the fact that just because we claim to be Christians does not mean we are immune to this kind of suffering.

So it comes as a chopping death-like blow to many Christian adults when they have to admit or face either their own or their child's emotional traumas. It is harder still to try to examine the causes or to dig up the ugly roots.

In case your childhood memories are buried too deeply for you to locate immediately, let me give you some examples. These are hurts out of my own childhood and a sampling from those of a great many other Christian adults. All of these conflicts have given their own measure of suffering. I may have missed your particular experiences, but perhaps you can in some way identify.

You may have lived your childhood and young adult life with one, several, or (I pray not) all of these things:

• The death, divorce, or mere absence of one or both parents.

• The complete or partial lack of support, approval, or verbal encouragement from parents or family which has left you with little or no feelings of worth or value.

17

- The overprotective parent or family member who never let you pay for a mistake, fall on your face, or run out of money—all of which generally did nothing to prepare you for your adult life in the big city.
- The parent or family member who made the home a hellish prison and wrought anguish on each member.
- The spiritual lectures and judgments given hypocritically and without love which were pounded into you by parents, other relatives, Sunday school teachers, ministers, or church members—and which still sting your memory and have left you a spiritual pygmy.
- The confused, frustrated feelings generated by parents who demanded that you honor them as the Ten Commandments prescribed, but then lived fraudulent double lives unworthy of that respect.
- The person in your childhood who picked, nagged, harassed, or teased you unmercifully, all under the thin guise of humor but which left your soul badly damaged.
- The continual upheaval and insecure feelings caused by being a transient family, always on the move.
- The inferior feelings you had, in your early teens, because your face or body (or both) was not up to the flawless perfection of a Barbie or Ken doll.
- The continuation of low self-esteem even now as an adult.
- The times of being depressed because you were chronically ill during most of your childhood or you had a crippling or disfiguring major disease.
- The mother or father who would not or could not trust you, and so they continually made false accusations about you and your activities.
- Parents who fought openly or secretly and then tried to force you into taking sides.
- The sting of remembered nicknames of your childhood which has left you sensitive to what you are called still, to this day.
- The mother or father who told you, even reminded you daily, that you were an unplanned child, and so you grew up "knowing" you were an unwanted person.

• Parents whose behavior was rude, embarrassing, or downright hostile and unexplainable.

• Parents who never communicated love or approval to you while you were growing up, but who now talk proudly about you and take the credit for rearing such a successful offspring.

• The struggles of accepting and coping with a mentally retarded brother or sister or the equally frustrating problem of living with a talented person or mental genius in the family.

• The parent or family member who abused you—physically, by punishment turned brutal; sexually, by molestation or rape; or verbally, by an unending stream of devastating criticisms and put-downs.

There are, of course, many more types of emotional suffering, but these experiences, taken from your childhood and mine, are enough for us to examine now.

Bringing those hurts to the surface from the place within you where they now lie and looking at the sufferings of your soul may frighten you to death, but we need healing in these areas. We also need some kind of understanding of our past if we are to ease our frustrations with daily living.

Not long ago, as I was getting dressed in my motel room and preparing to speak at a luncheon, I felt a sharp pain in my chest and discovered an ugly red lump just under my breast.

After my speaking engagement, and later that night, the lump had expanded from the diameter of a penny to the size of a quarter. By the time I returned home two days later, it was hard to ignore because the hard, flaming red core was covering a good portion of my chest.

My doctor uttered his usual "Mmmm" and then said rather matter-of-factly, "It's a large, badly infected sebaceous cyst."

I remember feeling a brief moment of relief, for I had (as all women do) diagnosed it myself as a malignant tumor.

My relief was short-lived, however, because the doctor continued, "I think it's reached a head, so I'll have to cut it open, drain it, and pack it."

The compassionate nurse, one who has stood by our doctor's side for the better part of twenty years, bent close and whispered to me, "It's going to be rough. We can't give you any Novocain for pain as it spreads the infection." I would have flown off that table in a minute had she not outweighed me.

"You mean he's going to open me up here, right now, with nothing but a sharp knife?"

That afternoon I learned the hard reality of it in the worst way: a cyst that becomes infected needs a sharp knife to lance it and clean it out, packing material to let it drain, and new packing material each day until it is healed.

So it is with our storehouse of old, suppressed memories. Sometimes they lie buried in our minds for years, much like my cyst, never giving us too much grief. But then someone says something, or we say something, that triggers an unexpected response from us or them, or we behave in an unexplainable way, and the tiny pangs of hurt begin to be felt. The infection has begun.

Finally, when the circumstances of life become unbearable and reach a "head," it's time for cutting open the box of memories and draining out the odorous pus so that the wound can heal.

If our memories are allowed to fester within us, they can cripple each relationship we try to establish. They can paralyze us daily and, in some cases, permanently. From that same sebaceous cyst, I learned about the length of recovery. I thought that cyst would take forever to heal. But healing comes to us on its own time-table, and so it is with inner emotional healing.

Our inner healing is a little like forgiveness—it must be constantly updated. We do not experience healing in one second flat. It generally plods along like a tired old horse. We must not be impatient with God's inner healings.

Healing also takes many forms and shapes and indeed, like forgiveness, it sometimes has to be run through our computers daily.

These days, these stress-filled days, I have found myself caring a great deal about the memories and the mental health of Christians. I haven't always put such a high priority on a healthy mind. In fact, for a long time after my husband Dick and I became committed believers, I was contented and thrilled beyond belief that God would simply use us in spiritual ways of healing.

Dick's Sunday school teaching in the high school department, his witnessing in his quiet but powerful way at the bank, my singing and speaking—all of these things were being used of the Lord for others' spiritual health, and I truly thought that was enough.

However, that was before I talked with hundreds of Christians who were desperately trying to cope with difficult childhood memories or frustrating present-day situations with in-laws, grown children, and all sorts of other relationships.

My lack of interest in mental and emotional health also came before I took a good look at my own personal inner agonies: certainly long before I allowed myself to look deep within me, and even longer before I let Jesus do His mighty work of inner healing for my childhood infections.

Mental health—yours and mine—is a delicate, slippery, and mysterious subject. God and all of heaven have certainly had their share of my pestering them about it, but because God so truly understands the deep emotional suffering of His children, it is to Him that we must go for help and healing.

Lest you think I have eliminated all emotional hurts from my life and now live a carefree existence, let me hurry to set the record straight. I am still working through many inner conflicting memories, but I don't trudge down those dark tunnels alone. Jesus is ever present. Nor do I set the following guidelines down as the all-American-failproof-ten-easy-step plan, but rather as alternatives or handles that just may ease your troubled mind and help you to cope with life in this distressing world.

1. **With Jesus by your side, go back in time and memory to your childhood.** On a sheet of paper, list some of the hurtful, distasteful events of your childhood and name the people involved. Begin with small hurts and end with the most painful memories. Remember as you write that we all can write a list like this, but most of us will not want to.

I have found that when a person who hurt me in some way when I was a child does or says something now which opens the old wound—even though I am an adult—the pain is worse. I find, too, that generally I cannot immediately find a reason for his actions. However, I noticed a few years ago that when the pain was **intense enough,** I began to be willing to seek the Lord's face on it, and I wrote down my list—unbearable as it was—so that I could begin to sort it out. And it turned out to be my first step toward sanity and a sound mind.

Your list may be short, long, fairly painful, or heavily devastating; but putting it on paper for no one's eyes but yours and the Lord's is as therapeutic to the soul as a hot whirlpool bath is to tired, aching muscles.

2. **Still with Jesus by your side, place your finger on each event and name on the list. As you go down the list, ask the Lord to let you see these situations and relationships from His perspective.** This will not be easy, especially if you have been hurt deeply, but remember—nothing connected with growing ever is! Particularly ask the Lord to show you how limited, handicapped, or crippled those parents, family members, or other persons really were themselves.

We may never know what childhood traumas our parents or brothers or sisters faced when **they** were children. For instance, we may never find out what turned a loving, warm girl into an embittered mother who physically or verbally abuses her children. We may never hear what childhood horror changed a conscientious boy into a dropout husband and father. But chances are very good that they experienced great hurts and humiliations while they were growing up. Our parents and families may never be able to speak of them, but—believe me—emotional and physical suffering has been going on since Adam, Eve, and sin.

Since I have written **Mourning Song**, a book on death and dying, I have been asked to speak at several medical seminars attended by nurses. One of the first things I ask them to do is to mentally take off their pretty, starched caps and lay down their sophisticated scientific knowledge, and crawl into a hospital bed to see the world of medicine from a frightened, sick patient's viewpoint. Very often this exercise marks the awakening of a sense of compassion and empathy. Dozens of nurses have told me that this attempt to see the hospital from the patient's eyes has served as their initial lesson on compassionate patient relations.

We are attempting to gain the same kind of empathy when we ask God to give us His insight and perspective about the people and circumstances in our memories. Besides that, we are told in the New Testament to make allowances for one another's faults. Only love can do it; and sometimes because the hurt is so deep, only God's love channelled through us can do it.

3. **With Jesus still beside you, ask Him to show you how to use those haunting, childhood experiences and memories for God's glory, your own good, and for a reconciling relationship with others.**

Once when I was thinking about Bryan Leech's wonderful way with song lyrics, my mind remembered a line from his song "The Hiding Place."

> There is a hiding place,
> a strong protective space
> where God provides the grace
> to persevere.*

*Bryan Leech, "The Hiding Place" (Targana, Calif.: Fred Bock Music Co., n.d.). Used by permission.

I wondered how Bryan knew about the "strong protective space," and how he knew that God would "provide the grace to persevere." When I talked with him recently, I asked him, "Bryan, what type of bending did God do to you in your life to produce such right-on lyrics?"

His answer was not immediate, and during the momentary pause a small voice within me shouted, "Listen up, Joyce, this will be important."

When Bryan did answer, he said simply, "Oh, Joyce, the circumstances of my life are so disappointing."

For the rest of our conversation I felt the sharp edge of God's digging trowel. Bryan shared with me his childhood in England, his troubled parents, his leaving England to come to the strange land of America, his conversion, his loneliness, and his present circumstances, which can only be described as "Most disappointing."

By the end of our conversation, it took no ingenious insight on my part to sense that his remarkable, talented ability with words and music was forged out of the fires of inadequate people, disfigured and warped by their own experiences, and Bryan's circumstances, which would have caused most of us to retreat forever into some dark place, never to peep out. Yet Bryan writes, and he writes eloquently.

Isn't it strange that out of an emotionally impoverished childhood and a life full of setbacks and uneasy alliances, God has been able to turn Bryan's songwriting talents into incredible works of truth and beauty? That's terribly New Testament!

Just today I was reading Paul's account of the marvelous giving record of the Macedonian church. A verse that spoke poignantly about God's "growing methods" was where Paul wrote, "Now, my brothers, we must tell you about the grace that God has given to the Macedonian churches. Somehow, in the **most difficult circumstances**, their overflowing joy and the fact of being down to their last penny themselves, produced a magnificent concern for other people" (2 Cor. 8:1,2, Phillips, emphasis mine).

How beautifully J. B. Phillips translated that when he used the words "difficult circumstances . . . down to their last penny . . . produced a magnificent concern for other people."

Here again, we see that the very thing that most discourages us can be used of God to develop our talents, our giving abilities, and our concern for others. How like God to give us the grace to see the suffering of the people in our past and present in His perspective, and then to turn those very things into things like Bryan's songs.

Go back and look at David for a moment. Writing the incredible amount of quality poetry found in the Psalms must have demanded David's undivided attention, time, and a lot of hereto unexplored growth-producing suffering. Where did David get his literary ability? Was it not from all those lonely hours out on the hills with only sheep to keep him company?

Did God allow David's childhood to be lonely and hard on purpose? I certainly think so. In fact, I believe God allowed David to be rejected by his brothers in order to bring the boy into complete dependence on his God and to add greatly to his spiritual stature. And while it's true that we need the fellowship of other believers, the number one point of growing is to recognize our utter dependence on God.

It is highly possible that the cold, dark, frightening hillsides of David's youth were where the greatest Psalms were born and where the best of growing took place.

A friend of mine, who knows the painful and intimate details of my past very well, suggested to me that my motivation for writing twelve books in the last nine years was born out of my own "disappointing circumstances" as a child. The same friend also suggested that perhaps I should be extremely grateful for the hurts, rejections, and people-failures in my past, for they have made me the woman I am today.

25

His point is well taken. For instance, I have often said, "I would never wish or want a mother to lose a child"; but losing my own son David has developed my abilities to be sensitive to the bereavement of any mother, anywhere in the world. Perhaps the childhood traumas and disappointments we have lived through are the very instruments God is using to lift us from being ordinary, routine people to being extraordinarily gifted ones. Perhaps it's those very things that hurt us in the past that now enable us to reach out to others.

Bryan Leech said, "God takes the negative and turns it into a positive." How true, and how like God!

A few weeks ago, I received a letter from a precious woman who is in the process of transcribing my book **Fragrance of Beauty** into Braille. I wondered how she got started in that line of work, and near the end of her letter, she told me she had initially learned Braille to help her young grandson who is blind. I immediately thought "a negative has produced a positive," and then I wondered what the chances would have been of her learning Braille had her grandson been blessed with 20/20 vision.

I wonder, too, if Peter—who had a great deal to say about suffering—might just have been zeroing in on emotional and mental suffering when he wrote, "After you have suffered a little while, Our God, who is full of kindness through Christ, will give you his eternal glory" (1 Pet. 5:10a TLB).

Point No. 1. Our suffering will give us not only pain but glory! "He personally will come and pick you up. . . ."

Point No. 2. God visits those who suffer—perhaps more than those who do not! "And set you firmly in place. . . ."

Point No. 3. I don't have to worry about getting a place or losing it. "And make you stronger than ever" (1 Pet. 5:10b, TLB).

Point No. 4. Ah, so there is a reason for suffering after all!

The Modern Language translation of 1 Peter 5:10

says God uses suffering to (1) equip, (2) stabilize, (3) strengthen, and (4) forever establish us!

So as you go over your list, know that God is **very** capable of turning our disastrous childhood memories into His own positive, helpful experience. Who knows, maybe your greatest talent lies rooted in your greatest suffering?

4. **Now, turn to Jesus, look deeply into His eyes, and ask the hardest thing of all. Ask Him to help you accept His healing, to give you a forgiving spirit toward these people and events so that you can move on.** I wonder how often our past keeps us in limbo—neither regressing nor moving forward?

I wonder, too, how much energy is consumed by those of us who are continually trying to grab and reach for that which was unobtainable during our childhoods? Or, I sometimes consider how much time we waste rehashing and analyzing the past—refusing to accept God's forgiveness or healing—only to find we are still being hurt over and over again by the same old hurts.

I guess we optimistically hope our offending parents, family, or relatives will change and treat us differently. But in reality, those who have wounded us in childhood may be continuing to inflict wounds today, and we find the hurts continuing. Or worse, the very person who was responsible for so many conflicts dies, leaving our wounds hemorrhaging and our conflicts unresolved, and we are faced with a thousand grim regrets.

Open your whole heart and being to God's tender, healing touch. He is the only one who knows the extensiveness of your hurt and how to stop the bleeding. As I write this, God is continuing a healing process in me which He began a few years ago. I know firsthand that it can be done and that He is able!

I also need to tell you that while I am not totally well, I have left the intensive care ward and am definitely on my way to recovery. That does not mean the situations that have caused my pains have changed. Some people and some negative forces from my childhood remain **exactly** the same today. They have not changed, nor do I expect or hope they will. But **I have changed.** I have begun to accept the Great Physician's work, and healing is happening.

With God's help we can claim Ephesians 4:32: "Instead, be kind to each other, tenderhearted, forgiving one another, just as God has forgiven you because you belong to Christ." (TLB). Especially we can claim the last part about the **way** to forgive and accept others. We can forgive them as God has beautifully forgiven us.

Hannah More wrote these words of wisdom: "A Christian will find it cheaper to pardon than to resent. Forgiveness saves the expense of anger, the cost of hatred, and the waste of spirits." It is this "waste of spirits" or waste of creative abilities that really concerns me when I talk to a person who **will not** forgive family or background.

I hope I am not making this sound too simple and easy, for I know only too well that it is not. But I know God! I know firsthand that God can ease our attitudes into acceptance.

Joseph, whose real-life experiences read like a soap opera and horror story all rolled into one, is a perfect example of what God can do with our past experiences. Special to my heart is the information that after Joseph was made second in command of Egypt, God blessed him with two sons, and I find their names highly significant.

Genesis 41:51,52 records, "Joseph named his oldest son Manasseh (meaning, 'Made to Forget'—what he meant was that God had made up to him for all the anguish of his youth and for the loss of his father's home). The second boy was named Ephraim (meaning 'Fruitful'—'For God has made me fruitful in this land of my slavery,' he said)" (TLB).

We may never get completely over the traumas of the past, but like Joseph we can, with God's gentle leading, begin to heal and move into being the free, real, and loving people God had in mind all along.

Think of it: even though He knew our parents, our

families, and the illogical and disturbing circumstances of our lives, God not only chose us, He accepted us! And then, read this:

Long ago, even before he made the world, God chose us to be his very own, through what Christ would do for us; he decided then to make us holy in his eyes, without a single fault—we who stand before him covered with his love. His unchanging plan has always been to adopt us into his own family by sending Jesus Christ to die for us (Eph. 1:4,5 TLB).

And He did this because He wanted to!

No matter what kind of family life we have endured or enjoyed, God's plan was to adopt us into His family —the perfect family, with no variances, no hurts, and no disappointments!

Reread these verses in Ephesians, and then tune your ear to the voice of God as He whispers down the canyons of your mind, "My child, you are loved, you are wanted, and you belong to Me! My love is breaking the fetters that bind you, so move out. Be real and loving, from this moment on, for you are My own chosen one, and a member of My family!"

Chapter Three

Growing Through Pain

> Out of suffering have emerged the strongest
> souls and
> The most massive characters are seamed
> with scars—
>
> —Edwin Hubbell Chapin

Pain and illness mean heartbreak, even if we have strong faith in the Lord. To nonchalantly say, "If you truly know Christ, pain will never get to you" is sheer madness.

Lazarus' illness and death broke the hearts of Martha and Mary, and of Jesus Himself; and He wept with the awful reality of it.

We must be careful when we dismiss pain as being "all in your head," and we must not give glib mini-sermons based on one verse of Scripture that presume to sufficiently deal with the age-old problem of pain. What is very hard to grasp about pain is the simple truth that it is **not** God's will to banish all disease, pain, or death in this **present** age.

I cannot buy the theory that Jesus wants everybody well. If He did, then no real born-again Christian would ever catch a cold or cancer, much less die. This present world is a melee of pain and death, and we must not confuse this world with the sin-free world to come. For now, here on this earth, we have no escape from trials, tragedies, and tears; so how do we cope with the pain of life?

I have been learning much about pain and, while the growing process is rough, it has been quite an eye-

31

opener. I've found that rarely do we like pain or understand its wild ride through our lives. And never have I known one single person who enjoyed pain or looked forward to it.

Yet, here and there, I am meeting men and women of high integrity and maturity. Sometimes their faces are pinched with pain, but their souls beat with a steady, unshakeable joy. They possess that undeniable yet unfathomable peace, and so help me, they glow!

I was pretty sure, at the outset of a painful condition in my jaw four years ago, that the pain would eventually kill all my joy, fade my peace, and certainly erase any glow I might have had. The realization of what pain was doing to me triggered a burning desire to search out how those who glowed with joy and peace in spite of their pain did so.

Let me back up a moment to say that along with the usual (and sometimes unusual) emotional pain of my past, the progress of my childhood was often hindered by some kind of physical illness. There were very few school semesters during which sickness did not present lengthy interruptions to my education. But hard physical pain, the kind I now know, did not begin its nightmarish existence until four years ago.

It seems to me I have been singing all my life. I started at age three, got very serious at thirteen, and have sung daily ever since.

Several years ago, during the recording session for the album "Joyce," I was quite taken back by how painful those sessions were to my throat. For hours afterwards, my throat, ears, eyes, and whole head ached beyond belief. I simply chalked the pain up to the tremendous stress a recording session always produces, and tried to let it go at that.

However, in the following months I became aware of an emerging pattern of pain that followed every concert or speaking engagement I gave. Again, I kept telling myself it was just stress, and I felt that if I could rest, the trouble would clear itself up.

Then four years ago, after speaking for a Family

Forum seminar in Colorado Springs I awakened in my motel room out of a sound sleep. It was three o'clock in the morning and I had a pain that I couldn't explain away or ignore.

The pain's highest intensity was in my mouth, and I was experiencing the worst toothache I had ever had. Not only was it painful, but it was also ridiculously frustrating because where the pain hurt the worst there was no tooth.

Nothing I took or did even touched the blinding hurt. It simply blossomed into an "all-teeth" ache, earache, and full-fledged migraine headache; and it pounded its message into me for the rest of the weekend. Exhausted and completely bewildered, I returned home and poured out my story to Dick. Though we didn't know it then, we were about to see just how hot the fiery furnace of pain can really get.

We also did not begin to estimate our growth in Christ, or how this emerging pain would forever change our lives.

When pain enters your life, the first practical and logical step is to pray, and so we did. We prayed for healing and wisdom. I am sure God heard us, but He decided to usher us into His waiting room.

Then, because we got bored with waiting and because God gave physicians brains and medical skills, we sought out some doctors to see if they could find the cause of my pain. It wasn't that we were running ahead of God. We had prayed for healing (nothing happened), but we had also prayed for wisdom; and common sense said we had "to do" something.

After head, ear, nose, and throat specialists ruled out any major problems, it came down to teeth and, finally (as our dentist discovered), my jaw.

Even though the tears were streaming down my face as I sat in the dentist's chair, I was very relieved that something was found to be wrong. I was beginning to suspect that this whole problem of pain was a psychosomatic situation and a figment of my imagination. My sense of humor had vanished, and I wasn't up to appreciating such remarks as "It's all in your head, Honey" because it literally **was** in my head. At least I sure thought so! The pain had become more than an after-concert nuisance—it was coming on daily.

Our family dentist sent me to a specialist, and he confirmed the jaw-joint diagnosis. He found my temporomandibular (jaw) joint in great trauma and began the first of what seemed like endless hours of work inside my mouth.

It seems that during my teen years several back molar teeth were removed, never replaced, and back tooth support was lost. This and other factors have allowed excessive pressure to be put on the jaw. Then, because head, jaw, and shoulder muscles are all inter-related, whenever there is an imbalance, all the muscles are affected and hence the pain.

Now—four years, much excellent dentistry, several thousand dollars, and many prayers and "why" questions later—almost everything that could be done has been done.

The good news: I am not in acute pain every day as I once was. However . . .

The bad news: anything from yawning, eating, and laughing to singing and speaking can still set off a twenty-four- to forty-eight-hour pain spree that is simply wild!

You've heard of the woman who talked so much her mouth wore out? Well, I've done it.

I can joke about it now because the pain I'm in today has been very minimal, but let me risk exposure and show you a small glimpse of my thoughts when pain was really controlling me and when my sense of humor was nonexistent.

I was sitting in the Sea-Tac Airport in Washington, in great pain, when I scribbled the following frag-mented thoughts on my yellow legal pad of paper.

People are swirling around me, catching planes, col-lecting luggage, and doing all the nervous things they do in airports.

But it's hard to focus.

Pain is a super-conceited monster who demands, and gets, my undivided attention.

Its huge shape blocks all the people, places, and emotions from my view.

It forces everything out of my mind and commands me to concentrate on its own intensity.

I will not give in to it! But I'm losing my grip.

The sun outside, behind the large expanse of glass windows, has just set and the clouds are gray against a fading pink sky. It's really lovely, and the Seattle-Tacoma waterways are reflecting the delicate pink. Momentarily, I am filled with the gentleness of the evening; but not for long. The beauty does not dull the ever-increasing, throbbing pain.

I haven't even begun my speaking engagement, and I'm already in pain.

Lord, could I go home? If I have to have pain, could I at least be surrounded by loving and familiar people and things?

The dark gray clouds of evening outside have somehow crept inside of me, and now they are clinging to the edges of my soul.

I'm beginning to feel swallowed up by their slimy, wet presence.

Clouds of depression always look and feel this way; thick, wet, and dark.

Is the sun warm and shining anywhere right now?

I don't think so.

Reason begs me to reconsider and alter my "poor me" attitude, but pain wipes logic off my mind's surface, and I'm convinced the whole world is wrapped and wadded up in this cloud of depression.

I can hear those of you who have not experienced prolonged or chronic pain cheerfully advising me to "look on the bright side" or "to remember God's promises" or "to think about something else." Henry G. Bohn once said, "He preaches patience that never knew pain."

At the same time I can see those of you who have

suffered nodding your heads in perfect agreement. My words make sense to you because you've been there. Perhaps your pain has been far more severe, far more debilitating, or has lasted far longer than mine; but we speak the same language, and we are on the same level of understanding.

For those of you who are really hurting right now, I would like to share some insights that have shed light on the problems of pain and have eased my heart on the blackest of pain-filled nights.

The most obvious lesson we all learn from pain is that it truly forces us to trust, and thus to grow. Either we respond to it and blossom, or we run the opposite way, shrivel up, and die. But facing up to our pain is always brutally hard, for the most obvious dilemma of pain is the ancient question **Why?**

Is having pain in our lives really allowed by God? Could God, in all good conscience, do such a shocking thing? And what's more, does God ever really use pain in a positive way?

Early in my pain, four years ago—or sitting in Sea-Tac Airport that day—I would have shouted, **"Absolutely not! God does not allow us to be destroyed by pain!"**

But because of some courageous suffering people, some startling few books, and some lovely but firm times of God's guiding hand, I now make the following statement:

I hate pain and suffering in any shape or form. I despise the finger of pain that has painted purple shadows beneath my eyes. I cringe when pain carves lines into my face with its sharp knife. I weep when pain capriciously flys away for a short spell, leaving me exhausted, drained, and of very little use to anyone.

But . . .

Pain has caused me to grow. I have earned my master's degree in "coping" from the high-priced school of pain, and I have seen my husband and children become giants in the faith.

I refuse to run from pain any longer. I still do not like it, but God has definitely brought pain into my life; and while I personally think it is the most difficult of all ways to grow, it certainly is very sure.

Here are some of the most tangible lessons God has taught me through my experiences with pain. They may not be the exact lessons you have learned, and they may not ease your heart completely. Your pain and questioning heart may only be answered in God's own original way, but I hope these words of mine pour some soothing ointment directly to the hurting part of you.

The Communion of Pain

The loneliness of pain has caused me to call my daughter or daughter-in-love and say, "I'm in such terrible pain today, I can't do anything here. How about going window shopping with me?" And often I have been able to crash through pain's lonely barrier for a few hours at least.

So, when in pain we turn to others to find communion. During the past four years I have read everything having anything to do with pain, and I have talked with hundreds of people about pain—either their own or a loved one's. When I wasn't in extreme pain, I looked carefully at the whys of pain, the healing of it, and the continuance of it.

Each time Dick and I prayed for the Lord to heal my jaw, and we do believe in divine healing, the Lord's answer was the same—not now. Even this afternoon I asked again and heard the same familiar response.

This has been the most difficult answer God has ever handed down to me, yet either I believe He knows what He is doing and that He is in complete control of my life, or I don't. Either I am willing to accept this pain as His will, or I am not.

I have always felt that if I could gain some insights

37

on pain, the acceptance would be a little easier. So I began a search for not just the "why" of pain but for the "how" of coping with continuous or chronic pain.

I'm not sure if I can adequately share all my findings regarding pain because aside from the physical beating it brings, it is also a highly emotional issue.

Pain to me is a very real person, and I can see his face quite clearly in my mind's eye. Quite simply, I hate him, and that should give you an idea of how emotional I am over this.

If you, dear reader, have ever suffered even a fair amount of physical pain, you know too well that people (even pastors, doctors, and counselors) who have experienced very little pain firsthand and thereby are calloused to the work of pain, seem to come out of the woodwork to surround and advise you. The man called Pain is nowhere near as real to them as he is to those who have languished under his whippings. Yet these cheerful, unpained souls become veritable towers of advice and expertise.

They tend—

    to find instant solutions,

    to claim instant healings,

    to find instant examples of our poor diet or lack of proper vitamin intake,

    to know in an instant what spiritual blockage is holding up our progress,

    to freely share their instant spiritual and medical diagnosis.

But, worst of all, they tend

    to instantly reacquaint us with the stench of phony advice, and there is no communion between us.

Your church and mine has its percentage of people whose pain-free existences have taught them that no pain is too great or too overwhelming for them to handle with a little help from God. While I understand their well-meaning and sincere attitude, I am convinced they are sincerely wrong: and this is why I am speaking out so strongly.

People in pain do not need one more painful thing in their lives.

Gordon McAllister, a young man who has survived five brain surgeries and now lives with yet another tumor quietly resting against his brain, said, "Some Christians actually torture those in pain by the thoughtless things they say."

Over the past years I've received my share of unsolicited and less-than-helpful advice. Much has come by mail, some by phone, some in personal encounters, and a few disheartening times by sermons in church.

But little or no communion came with those contacts, and the feeling that I would forever endure this pain alone began to strangle me. About the time I thought I had been abandoned and was frustrated the most about my pain, it occurred to me that perhaps I should change the specifics of my prayers. Instead of bombarding heaven with requests—no, **demands** is a more accurate term—for my immediate healing, I decided to stop asking and begin listening.

Once more I heard the still, small voice say, "Not now," and so I quite badgering the Lord about healing. I admit to mentioning it every now and then, however, because I love the verse, "Ye have not because ye ask not." However, mostly I'm quiet about my personal healing.

I began to pray about my encounters with people. I told Him I was lonely and dreamed of having communion with Him and some earthly being who would understand. I asked God to place in my path people who had grown because of pain. I dearly longed to hear their godly, experiential advice. I also asked Him to lead me to books and sermons that would heal the inner questions and hurts.

Slowly it began to dawn on me that there were people around who, unlike the physically well "advice givers" had suffered with cataclysmic pain. These were people who would have something very valid and very healing to say to me, and so I prayed in earnest and began to search them out.

The Lord answered those prayers and He moved—slowly at first—to turn my face, heart, and mind in their direction. It was as if the Lord Himself slipped a few drops of His own quiet confidence into my coffee cup one morning, and while the pain was not erased, I felt that out in the big bad world somewhere was a person, a book, a letter, or a sermon that would teach me about living with this monster named Pain. It was my first measure of hope.

As I have learned to pray not for healing but for opportunities to learn, my insights and sensitivities have really been sharpened to a razor's fine edge. For instance, whenever I pick up a book dealing with pain or talk even briefly with someone about the problems of pain, I can tell almost instantly if the writer or speaker has gone to the school of pain or is merely an over-the-wall observer. We either take communion together or we don't.

The people acquainted with suffering have this in common: they **rarely** give quick, pat answers. And when they speak, I am aware of the expense and the high cost of their marvelous wisdom.

Those who suffer also have something else in common: they always touch and soothe the spot deep inside me that hurts the most. They have the genuine gift of comforting others.

Years ago, just before we lost our infant son David, our friend Al Sanders introduced me to the books of Martha Snell Nicholson. What a marvelous comfort her words have been! But no one, not even our gifted and sensitive friend Al, could have guessed the communion between her words and my pain, or what those books would bring to me these past months.

Mrs. Nicholson had five major diseases. She was confined to her bed, unable to move anything but her feet and hands, and in constant pain. Yet in a book no longer in print, she said, "Every morning I awake with quick wonder in my heart and wonder what bright new gift He will give me today."

Her struggle with pain taught her many lessons, but

her poem "When He Putteth Forth His Own Sheep, He Goeth Before Them" records how she coped with the loneliness pain produces. The words take on special meaning when you realize the poem was written after her doctor wrote on his report, "Case too far advanced to respond to treatment."

I could not walk this darkening path of pain alone.
The years have taken toll of me;
Sometimes my banners droop, my arms have grown too
    tired,
And laughter comes less easily.

And often these my shrinking cowardly eyes refuse
To face the thing that is ahead of me,
The certainty of growing pain and helplessness . . .
But O, my Lord is good, for He

Comes quickly to me as I lie there in the dust
Of my defeat and shame and fear.
He stoops and raises me, and sets me on my feet,
And softly whispers in my ear

That He will never leave me—nay, that He will go
Before me all the way. And so,
My hand in His, along this brightening path of pain,
My Lord and I together go!*

Dr. Ralph Byron, a surgeon at City of Hope Hospital, once said that the greatest fear a cancer patient experiences is that at some point in time he will be abandoned. Mrs. Nicholson's poem pushes through that great fear by giving us hope in the words "My Lord and I together go!"

Her response to pain is in the following poem. We who have suffered know all too well about the kind of exhaustion described here.

*Martha Snell Nicholson, Heart Held High (Chicago, Ill.: Moody Press, 1954). Used by permission.

IN A HOSPITAL

Too tired to think, Lord,
Too tired to pray.
Words come so hard, Lord,
What could I say?

Too tired to feel, Lord,
Aught but this pain.
Through what long nights, Lord,
Here I have lain!

Sometime I'll work, Lord,
Sometime I'll pray,
Praise and adore Thee,
But not today.

Blessed assurance,
He understands.
Just let me rest, Lord,
Safe in Thy hands.*

Relating to honest words like these comes very easily. If you have experienced prolonged pain, you will remember how difficult it is to pray. How I loved Mrs. Nicholson's refreshing words. She didn't pick up a heavy bag of guilt for being too tired to pray; she simply accepted it as the way of pain. Then she trusted God's understanding heart and rested in His love. How beautiful!

Mrs. Nicholson also knew exactly how we would despise pain, but she longed for us to prepare ourselves for its eventuality and existence.

Her analogy of pain being a river into which a child dips his feet is a masterpiece of teaching. She called it,

*Martha Snell Nicholson, Heart Held High (Chicago, Ill.: Moody Press, 1954). Used by permission.

FIRST SUFFERING

Pain is a river, and today
My very little Sweet,
Into its dark and turgid depths
You dipped your small white feet.

It was the first time you had felt
The touch of grief or woe;
You shrank from it and wept; and yet,
Dear heart, you had to know

Though pain is part of life, our God
Makes bitter waters sweet—
You took a step toward heaven when
In pain you dipped your feet.*

From the communion of her writings, I have seen so clearly that healing very well may not be God's will. Only my will would claim healing; but so often God's will chooses to use pain, **not** healing, to do His work.

Would Mrs. Nicholson's poems have soothed my heart and drunk communion with me today if they had not been written out of pain? I doubt it. Yet, I'm sure she longed for instant healing. I rejoice that she accepted her suffering, wrote in all honesty about it, and was willing to share what the Lord was teaching her.

Though Mrs. Nicholson has been with the Lord for some twenty years now, her words still find communion with my soul, and over and over again I am drawn back to her choice books of poetic love.

Since I have prayed for encounters with people and books, the Lord has not only reminded me of past helps, like Mrs. Nicholson's work, but He has dropped into my lap very present-day people and writings.

I remember one night not long ago when I had given

*Martha Snell Nicholson, **Heart Held High** (Chicago, Ill.: Moody Press, 1954). Used by permission.

43

up eating dinner because the pain in my jaw was so acute. I was unable to disguise the level of pain, and so my face registered the full force of it. Dick eventually lost his appetite, and we dragged ourselves through the evening. By 9:00 P.M. we simply sat on the couch together—not talking, watching TV, or reading, but just sitting there—when our doorbell rang. Dick answered it, but I didn't have the strength nor the hospitality to get up. In fact I didn't even look up until both Mary and Keith Korstjens were in the room before me. (Mary is my "millionaire" friend who is paralyzed with polio and about whom I wrote in **The Richest Lady in Town.** Her husband, Keith, is our dear friend too and one of our pastors.)

Keith pushed Mary's wheelchair to Dick's side, and then he dropped to his knees in front of me. He took my hands in his, put his head on my lap, and wept.

No one called them, no one set up the appointment, no one told them I was in deep pain; but as they were driving home earlier that evening, they both knew they should stop by the Landorfs'.

After Keith slowed down his tears, he simply poured his heart out to the Lord. He voiced all the "why" questions I had screamed within my heart. He spoke honestly of his inability to make any sense out of all of this, and, in a very gentle way, he reminded God of His promises in the Word.

My pain did not go away or even ease, but the four of us and Jesus Himself took communion together that night, and I shall never ever be the same again.

As my family and friends have been drawn into this involvement with pain, the cords of love have grown between us and have strangely bound our hearts together. Our daughter Laurie has not only prayed with and for me, but has merely sat and cried with me. No money can buy that kind of gift.

My daughter-in-love Teresa once told me that whenever I was in severe pain on Rick's day off, he would stop whatever he was doing once an hour and pray for me. I'm sure my pain has given rise to some in-depth power in his prayer life. Even today, Teresa's dear voice said over the phone, "We'll be praying."

I have felt the presence and power of my sister's and father's prayers in spite of the fact that both live far from me.

But the communion pain has wrought between Dick and me has been the sweetest. Over and over I have lain back my aching head while he repeatedly applied the steaming hot towels to my face, and I've cried with love as he whispered, "Oh, Joyce, if only I could have this pain for you."

While it's true that pain can come slamming down like a wedge of steel between two people in a marriage, it is also true that God can use pain as His own special velvet cords of love to bind a marriage firmly together.

Every once in awhile I have to remind myself that were it not for this hideous pain, I would know nothing of this kind of communion with Jesus and others.

The Compassion of Pain

Over the last four years I've become aware of a curious phenomenon happening in my speaking engagements and during my personal conversations with people.

I can be speaking to an audience of five hundred people or of just a few, but very quietly and clearly I can spot and zero in on the person who is hurting the most.

"Whom have you lost?" I asked the lady in front of me.

"My father and sister," she answered, and then added, "How did you know?"

I told her I didn't know about her father or sister, but I saw pain and loss written across her face.

Before me, from my file on pain, is a letter from that same woman. Her note to me begins with the words,

"I am the lady with the 'look of pain' you saw and spoke to on Friday the 19th of September at the Christian Writers' Conference held at the Marriott Hotel."

In my mind's eye I can see her face yet. Her letter confirms some very real and frightening fears she was experiencing and she ends by thanking me for being such a sensitive person.

Would I be so alert to the hidden hurts and submerged suffering of others if I had not felt the icy fingers of pain in my own soul? I doubt it. And this kind of an encounter is happening to me over and over again.

I now realize that my mother was able to do the same kind of thing in the years before she died. She always made a beeline for someone in a room full of people, and nine times out of ten it was a person who was desperately troubled, hurting, and needing her. I used to think her instant rapport with hurting people was because God had given her the gift of discernment. Maybe He gave her that too, but now I'm more inclined to think it was her own ever-growing battle with the pain of breast cancer and her willingness to let God use it. Her pain led her into instant compassion for others.

It seems to me that once we have experienced any type of bout with pain, especially prolonged pain, we will have no trouble recognizing it in someone else's eyes. But this is only true if we ask God to use our pain to His glory.

We all have known people who have experienced great pain but have never asked the Lord to use it and so they have become bitter; they are forever whining or complaining. They not only offer no compassion to those in pain, but they are very difficult to be around.

David the psalmist said, "It is good for me that I have been afflicted; that I might learn thy statutes" (Ps. 119:71, KJV). It seems he needed a reason for his pain, just as we do; and **without** complaining, he asked for lessons from the Lord.

David learned those lessons well, for when we are really suffering, how often do we turn to the Psalms?

Almost always because David had been deeply hurt and God was able to translate his pain into compassion for others.

Long after David wrote the Psalms, Paul wrote to the Thessalonians, "For he [God] is using your sufferings to make you ready for his kingdom . . ." (2 Thess. 1:5, TLB).

As I mentioned earlier, I have read everything I can find on suffering, pain, and healing. The other day I picked up a small book that dealt with the "whys" of pain.

The author did an incredible thing. He reduced the problems of pain to four simple points:

1. There is no reason for pain and so I should not look for one.
2. I should accept pain. Period.
3. I should memorize and claim Romans 8:28.
4. Then, I would "know" that all pain is ultimately for my good.

The author's conclusions taught me one thing—he has never in all of his life suffered much more than an infected hangnail! Or if by some chance he has suffered, I know he never asked God to teach him how to really use it.

I was not comforted, enlightened, or helped by that book—only disgusted. Later, I had to ask the Lord's forgiveness for my rotten attitude because the man, through no fault of his own, wrote out of good intentions. However, we who have suffered could not have communion with that author; and he, because he knew no reason for suffering, could offer no words of compassion.

About the same time I flung his book down in despair, my friend Sally sent me Rev. Charles Swindoll's newest book, **For Those Who Hurt.** Since Chuck Swindoll is no stranger to me and had already been used of God in my life regarding pain I eagerly read his book. The unbelievable difference between Chuck's book and the other one was almost humorous.

Both books dealt with the whys of pain; both were

47

beautifully and rightly based on Scripture; both were about the same number of pages in length; but, while one book said almost nothing, Chuck Swindoll's book said **everything.**

I phoned him.

"Do you know what I really like about your book, Chuck?" I was almost shouting. "There is not one single cliché in the whole thing! How and what produced such a marvelous, truthful book?" I asked.

Then, for the better part of an hour, Chuck gave me a rather quick but intense biographical sketch of his childhood traumas, his emotional pain during adolescence, the physical pain of family members, and in general, the hurts of his own heart.

No wonder his rare book reaches out and embraces me with compassion. We have walked the same roads, fallen in the same valleys, and reached the same astonishing conclusions: one of the ministries of pain is to give us the ability to comfort others in **their** pain.

How else can God do what He promised? He said He would be our comfort, but how is this realistically possible unless God comforts **through** us?

This is exactly how the book **For Those Who Hurt** was born.

The book was first preached and then written because a couple of years ago Chuck looked over his pulpit and accurately read the facial expressions of one of the men seated in the congregation. The man seemed to be disintegrating with his hurt because his daughter had just run away from home for the seventeenth time.

"When I saw how deeply this father was hurting," Chuck told me, "I asked God to give me a message that would heal his hurt and answer the need of his brokenness. After dinner that night I wrote the sermon and later the book about 2 Corinthians 1:3–11."

I am predicting that Rev. Charles Swindoll's relevant little book, borne out of the compassion of a sufferer, will be mightily used of God. That's an easy prediction because it takes one in pain to know one. Often when we ask God to really use us, He draws on the most painful experience of our lives and turns it into honest compassion.

Read again that familiar passage by Paul, 2 Corinthians 1:3–11:

What a wonderful God we have—he is the Father of our Lord Jesus Christ, the source of every mercy, and the one who so wonderfully comforts and strengthens us in our hardships and trials. And why does he do this? So that when others are troubled, needing our sympathy and encouragement, we can pass on to them this same help and comfort God has given us. You can be sure that the more we undergo sufferings for Christ, the more he will shower us with his comfort and encouragement. We are in deep trouble for bringing you God's comfort and salvation. But in our trouble God has comforted us—and this, too, to help you: to show you from our personal experience how God will tenderly comfort you when you undergo these same sufferings. He will give you the strength to endure.

I think you ought to know, dear brothers, about the hard time we went through in Asia. We were really crushed and overwhelmed, and feared we would never live through it. We felt we were doomed to die and saw how powerless we were to help ourselves; but that was good, for then we put everything into the hands of God, who alone could save us, for he can even raise the dead. And he did help us, and saved us from a terrible death; yes, and we expect him to do it again and again. But you must help us too, by praying for us. For much thanks and praise will go to God from you who see his wonderful answers to your prayers for our safety! (TLB).

We suffer pain and hurt as God allows it, but we never suffer needlessly. No! Our suffering prepares us as nothing else can to identify and recognize pain in others and to comfort with wisdom and tenderness.

About the time I was wondering how my pain would ever produce compassion in me, I received this letter from Dr. Keith Korstjens, my friend who has wept and prayed for me over the years. His letter said, in part,

49

These past weeks I have asked the Lord so many times to give some explanation for the awful pain you have been enduring.

It's so human to want to know the "whys" of His workings. At any rate, what He has told me so far is probably not new to you at all. You have known, or at least expected, this for some time now. It's nothing spectacular, yet it helps me put your present hardship into some kind of focus. It's just this:

Your books have each come out of great personal and deep experience. Sometime in the future you will write to help the one who endures great **physical** pain.

His Stubborn Love speaks to heartbreak; **Mourning Song** helps the one with turbulent feelings about death; **The Richest Lady in Town** addresses itself to a hundred or more common inappropriate attitudes that plague our daily lives.

Someday a book by you will speak to the thousands who suffer physical pain but do not understand why.

I pray, dear Keith, this is the book.

The Sharing of Pain

The concept of "sharing pain" is difficult to grasp, yet Scripture confronts us with this idea over and over again.

Remember earlier when I wrote about emotional pain? I said that as believers we are part of God's family. Read what Paul said we should expect because of our family ties:

> And so we should not be like cringing, fearful slaves, but we should behave like God's very own children, adopted into the bosom of his family, and calling to him, "Father, Father." For his Holy Spirit speaks to us deep in our hearts, and tells us that we really are God's children. And since we are his children, we will share his treasures—for all God gives to his Son Jesus is now ours too. But if we are to share his glory, we must also share his suffering (Rom. 8:15–17, TLB).

In 2 Corinthians 1:7, Paul referred to those who are "partakers of the sufferings." And to the Christians at Philippi, Paul wrote, "For to you has been given the privilege not only of trusting him but also **suffering** for him" (Phil. 1:29, TLB, emphasis mine).

In that same letter he wrote, "That I may know him, and the power of his resurrection, and the **fellowship** of his sufferings . . ." (Phil. 3:10, KJV, emphasis mine).

In a letter to Timothy, Paul said,

I am comforted by this truth, that when we suffer and die for Christ it only means that we will begin living with him in heaven. And if we think that our present service for him is hard, just remember that some day we are going to sit with him and rule with him. But if we give up when we suffer, and turn against Christ, then he must turn against us. Even when we are too weak to have any faith left, he remains faithful to us, for he cannot disown us who are part of himself, and he will always carry out his promises to us (2 Tim. 2:11-13, TLB).

Evidently, Paul was saying that if we refuse to share the Lord's suffering, we will be faced with joyless consequences.

Peter's words do the most to convince me that sharing in the Lord's suffering is part of the Christian's upbringing. I can hear Peter's deep and resonant voice, mellowed through time by the Holy Spirit, saying, "This suffering is all part of the work God has given you. Christ, who suffered for you, is your example. Follow in his steps" (1 Pet. 2:21, TLB).

Probably his most precious words of encouragement are found in this passage:

Dear friends, don't be bewildered or surprised when you go through the fiery trials ahead, for this is no strange, unusual thing that is going to happen to you. Instead, be really glad—because these trials will make

51

you partners with Christ in his suffering, and afterwards you will have the wonderful joy of sharing his glory in that coming day when it will be displayed. (1 Pet. 4:12, 13, TLB).

In other words, my attitude toward pain should be one of gladness because pain is the very thing that makes me "partners with Christ."

My friend Gordon, with brain surgeries behind him and a dormant tumor lying in his brain now, said wistfully to me, "I miss not being seriously ill." Since I had never heard anyone say such a thing, I questioned him about his statement.

He explained, "It's just that when I was about to have surgery, or when my tumors were growing incredibly fast and my very existence was in jeopardy, I was closer to the Lord than anytime I've ever known. I miss that."

The words of my friend Gordon and all these Scriptures have convinced me that although I can believe in the Great Physician's power to heal our pain-saturated lives, I must also realize that suffering is a lesson in sharing. That lesson is designed to teach us to eventually share in God's holy glory.

I have just finished writing a biblical novel on Martha. While doing my research, I was made especially aware of the nature of Jewish hopes and dreams.

The Jews desperately wanted and certainly felt they needed a **reigning** Messiah, but that is not what they got. Jesus came as a **suffering** Messiah and many Jews never understood that concept.

Neither do we, really. After all, we want Jesus to come into our lives like a great sovereign king and set everything in order. We expect Him to banish all pain and suffering from the kingdom. So when He comes and does **not** put an end to our pain but leads us **into** and **through** suffering, pain, and disappointments, we are as frustrated and confused as the Jewish patriarchs of long ago.

We halfheartedly say, "I guess the Lord knows why,

but I sure don't!" We have no concept of suffering with Jesus. Nor are we willing to see that we will never have a totally reigning Messiah in our earthly lifetime. We will fully know Jesus as sovereign King and Messiah only in heaven.

If I take time to reread the Bible's words on suffering, somehow the burden of pain is easier to bear, especially when I remember that Jesus and I share it together.

Charles Haddon Spurgeon once wrote, "As sure as God puts His children into the furnace of affliction, He will be with them in it!"

The Blessing of Pain

Could there be such a thing as a blessing in and during pain? Yes, and here are just three ways we experience those blessings:

(1) pain is temporary;
(2) pain can be creative; and
(3) Jesus really does provide the strength to endure.

One dear woman wrote to me after the death of her thirty-eight-year-old son and said in part, "We saw some **immediate** healings during his lifetime, but then we saw the **ultimate** healing of his death and home-going."

I find no conflict here. In many cases God does heal here and now—sometimes **immediately**—and our hearts long for this to happen; but other times, He uses the "ultimate" healing of a heaven-going experience. Still, pain is temporary if we look at it in the light of time and all eternity.

Just yesterday I talked with Linda whose little two-year-old daughter has a severely damaged brain. Although Amy is unable to do anything a healthy two-year-old can do, her mother said, "Oh, but Joyce, Amy's problems are temporary! So temporary! Some-day—maybe only after we reach heaven, but someday —Amy will be whole and well."

A hundred years ago a man, whose name has been forgotten, wrote of pain and said, "Pain is lent to us for just a little while that we may use it for eternal purposes. Then it will be taken away and everlasting joy will be our Father's gift to us, and the Lord will wipe all tears from off our faces."

Last year, when I was afraid this pain in my jaw was not temporary but permanent, the same friend who gave me Chuck Swindoll's book sent me one of his taped sermons.

I listened to Chuck's exposition of Romans 8:17–27 while I was driving on the freeway, and several times I nearly caused a pile-up. It's hard to cry and drive at the same time. But it was the first time I had put the concept of sharing Christ's suffering into the same box with my pain. It was this tape that caused me to search the Scriptures and formulate my opinions on sharing Christ's suffering.

Chuck also brought Romans 8:17–27 into a most meaningful focus in another way. He did not talk of Romans 8:28, that beautiful diamond of a verse, and I'm glad he didn't. I wasn't ready for it at that time. What he did say loudly and clearly was that I would have suffering, but it would be nothing compared to the glory God would give later.

In other words, my pain was temporary. What a truth to learn while experiencing a jaw ache!

I wrote a letter thanking Chuck for the message of his tape. I did not ask for or expect an answer from him, yet his reply was definitely of the Lord. He wrote,

Dear Joyce:

I'm touched.

Really.

Your moving, heartrending response grabbed my inner man like a vice. Little did I know my words would ever get back to you and be used to strengthen you.

It's about time! You've invested years in giving, my friend. I'm pleased God allowed you to **receive** some specially wrapped, carefully chosen words.

What is it Solomon calls them? Apples of gold in pictures of silver? He framed them just for . . . just for **you.**

Of course, your groaning and pain concern a host of us who love you, Joyce. Rest assured that none of us know why it hasn't been relieved.

And so . . . we wait with you.

Touched.

Really.

Your friend,

Charles R. Swindoll

His words, "And so . . . we wait with you," have tiptoed across my mind in the middle of one pain-filled day after another. Following always behind Chuck's words is the still, small voice of the Holy Spirit saying, "It won't be too much longer; this is only temporary, Joyce."

When I ask the Lord to heal these painful jaw joints and I hear His now familiar, "Not now," I can truly say it's easier to wait—knowing the blessing of pain is that it is temporary and that God gives me strength to endure.

Martha Snell Nicholson once wrote,

We are now His broken things. But remember how He used broken things, the broken pitchers of Gideon's little army, the broken roof through which the palsied man was lowered to be healed, and the broken alabaster box which shed its fragrance over the broken body of our Savior. Let us ask Him to take our broken hearts and to press upon them further suffering to give us a poignant realization of the suffering of all the world. Let us ask Him to show us the endless, hopeless river of lost souls. This will break our hearts anew; but when it happens, God can use us at last.*

"Now we are His broken things," she wrote, which implies that someday we will be made whole. This

*Martha Snell Nicholson, Heart Held High (Chicago, Ill.: Moody Press, 1954).

brokenness, used for God's purpose, is only temporary.

One other blessing of pain is its ability to force us to be creative. The first time I realized pain could be used in a creative way was when I read **The Mystery of Pain.** It was written by a pastor, Paul J. Lindell, who was dying of cancer. His book opened up a whole new door to my thinking on pain.

He wrote, "Pain can help to illuminate our calling!" When I read that sentence the first time it didn't make too much sense. Then I began to count some of the creative things that pain has really produced.

The emotional pain of a mongoloid child's life and death has produced Dale Evans' book **Angel Unaware.** The pain of five diseases forced Martha Snell Nicholson to write prose and poetry unparalleled in present-day writings. Studies have shown that the pain of childhood or present-day illness has, over and over again, produced miraculous and beautiful things in the lives of many highly successful people.

The best example of pain and suffering illuminating a calling is found in Jesus and the suffering He experienced on the cross.

The writer of Hebrews wrote, "Jesus . . . who for the joy that was set before him **endured** the cross . . ." (Heb. 12:2, KJV, emphasis mine).

Our Lord understood full well that the cross was one of the stipulations of His work on earth and part of His joy was a product of His pain. But He **endured,** and forgiveness for you and me was creatively brought into existence. What a Savior!

Just this past week, Lois Chilton, a returned missionary from the Philippines, told me of a girl named Martina.

Martina was young, beautiful, and very bright. She left the missionary compound in Manila to go up north and teach Bible classes in English and three other dialects.

Not too long after Martina was gone, she wrote Lois

and said she was experiencing a "funny numbness in her feet" and was coming down to Manila for some medical help. The doctors in Manila diagnosed her problem as the worst type of leprosy and gave her a very short life expectancy.

Lois said, "When we visited her at the leprosarium during the next few months, we could hardly bear to see her." Martina's beautiful face had crumbled and disintegrated very quickly. But God did an amazing thing. For even though Martina was dying, she organized and taught four Bible classes. God blessed her work so much that she was able to start a small church there on the grounds of the leprosarium. That church still goes on today.

Before Martina died and in one of her last letters to Lois, she wrote of all the exciting opportunities she had participated in and ended her letter with the words, "I praise God for the gift of leprosy!"

Pastor Lindell's words about pain could certainly be said of Martina. God sweetly taught her about the blessings of pain and in the process gave her a ministry which will go on past the borders of our time and will march right into eternity.

But how did Martina endure? How do any of us endure?

Paul told the Corinthians, ". . . God will tenderly comfort you when you undergo these same sufferings. He will give you the strength to endure" (2 Cor. 1:7, TLB).

The prophet Isaiah laid the responsibility on God's shoulders when he wrote, "He giveth power to the faint; and to them that have no might he increaseth strength." (Isa. 40:29, KJV).

Peter talked of pain's temporariness and how we will endure when he wrote, "After you have suffered a little while, our God, who is full of kindness through Christ, will give you his eternal glory. He personally will come and pick you up, and set you firmly in place, and make you stronger than ever" (1 Pet. 5:10, TLB).

Did you notice that there is no mention of suffering and pain being **totally over** or completely removed, but only that Jesus will

(1) come,
(2) pick us up,
(3) set us firmly in place, and
(4) make us stronger than ever.

Knowing that our suffering is temporary and that Jesus really understands and will pick us up and make us stronger than ever challenges my heart to want to say with Mrs. Nicholson:

Oh Lord, if pain will help me to know You and Your suffering better; if pain will bring a closeness not possible in good health; if pain will give me a creative healing ministry with other hurting people, then "press upon me further suffering," for I know the strength to endure will be mine.

In the meantime, in yesterday's mail, a dear lady wrote, "Isn't He wonderful! Stick in there, Joyce. Glory is just around the corner!" And, another letter from a Christian gentleman who had obviously experienced a great deal of pain reads,

So may I say that I know what you are going through. I have been and will continue to pray for you.

Remember Jesus said, "I will never leave Joyce or forsake her." (Heb. 13:5) I felt led to put your name in.

Sometimes people will not understand how you feel. So may I say look to Jesus for He knows and understands.

Enduring is a little more bearable with dear letters of the heart like these.

Then in today's mail, a new friend writes, "When I was having much pain, my husband gave me a tee shirt with a picture of a cat hanging onto a cross-bar, and a saying that says, 'Hang in there, Baby!' And that's what I say to you, dear one. I know the Lord will surely bless you as you continue to serve Him."

Telling someone to "hang in there, Baby!" might not sound too terribly spiritual to some of you, but to those of us in pain it translates Romans 8:17–27 and 2 Corinthians 1:3–11 into a most practical language.

While we wait with pain, we grow. Pain is an experience that is **never** wasted. Every pain is used by God and through our pain we begin to understand the meaning of communion with others, compassion for others, and sharing with Christ. And to our continued surprise, our blessings grow and we are like a field that is ready for harvest.

I do not know the author, but someone once wrote,

> Whatever, wherever I am,
> I can never be thrown away.
> If I am in sickness,
>   my sickness shall serve Him;
> In perplexity,
>   my perplexity may serve Him.
> If I am in sorrow,
>   my sorrow may serve Him.
> He does nothing in vain.
> He knows what He is about.

And I shout, "Yes, He knows what He is about and I will trust Him and hang in there!"

Chapter Four

Growing Through Obedience

To obey God in some things
and not in others,
Shows an unsound heart.

—Thomas Watson

The name of the airport's restaurant has long since blurred in my memory because there have been so many such places in my life; however, the conversation that took place there is still crystal clear.

The gifted psychologist Dr. Jim Dobson and I had just finished a three-day family seminar. We were both exhausted. If we could have poured our combined energy into a thimble, it would have barely wet the bottom. It was no time to ask Jim what made him grow spiritually; yet I was feeling a small pinch of guilt for lost opportunities in this direction. So in between bites of his chocolate fudge sundae and my stale apple pie, I said, "You know, Jim, I'm writing a book on how Christians grow, how they mature in life, and what really makes our Christian lives productive—so, how does God help you grow?"

I think he finished his sundae because I had time to push aside my pie, pick up my pen, fold over my placemat and get all set to record his answer by the time he had reflected on my question.

Jim's life and his entire family are a personal joy to Dick and me. His books—**Dare to Discipline, Hide or Seek, What Wives Wish Their Husbands Knew About Women,** and a couple of new ones—are all being mightily used of the Lord. He is what I would call a productive, fruitful Christian gentleman.

When he finally replied he said simply, "Chastisement and obedience."

Then (I suppose because his first book was on the balance between love and discipline) he quoted a passage from the twelfth chapter of Hebrews. I came home to read that passage over and over again. I am amazed at how this Scripture has widened the window of my perspective on the inner character of God. I include much of it here because not only does it reveal the character and nature of God, but also it lays down one of the main guidelines for producing growth through chastisement and obedience.

And have you forgotten the exhortation which addresses you as sons?—"My son, do not regard lightly the discipline of the Lord, nor lose courage when you are punished by him. For the Lord disciplines him whom he loves, and chastises every son whom he receives."

It is for discipline that you have to endure. God is treating you as sons; for what son is there whom his father does not discipline?

If you are left without discipline, in which all have participated, then you are illegitimate children and not sons (Heb. 12:5–8, RSV).

Later in that same chapter we are told that God disciplines us for our good so that we may share His holiness; and then it continues, "For the moment all discipline seems painful rather than pleasant; later it yields the peaceful fruit of righteousness to those who have been trained by it" (Heb. 12:11, RSV).

Evidently God is really serious when He calls us His children, and it is His desire to see us grow into adulthood. It would also seem that He intends to train and discipline us and that He expects us to be obedient children.

It would be lovely if all this growing could be accomplished without rules, lessons, and growing pains, but any thinking parent knows better.

Jim Dobson said that all through the Christian's walk it is as if God is whispering to us, telling us about the way that is best. Then the Lord's voice gets stronger and louder, and finally we hear Him saying, "This is what I want you to do; now you do it." And then we have to make a choice. We can choose to diligently obey or to knowingly disobey. It's up to us.

I have long surmised that all those beautiful fruits of the Spirit—love, joy, peace, patience, kindness, goodness, faithfulness, gentleness, and self-control—are **all** preceded by one continual procedure on our part: **obedience.**

I would like to have all nine of those attributes shining in my life like large klieg lights, but I'll have none of them if I am not willing to turn my will over to the Holy Spirit. Without my obedience, those fruits are as remote and unobtainable as the farthest planet in space.

Obedience is tough. It is a continuing process, a daily thing, and to obey means conforming to God's will—**not ours.**

How often have I said, "I know what God wants me to do in this matter, but I am not willing to do it." The sad thing is that when those efforts of mine end in frustrating failure, I rarely remember that it was my **deliberate choice** to ignore God's will that determined the outcome.

I have taken several classes from Dr. William Glasser, M.D., and I've read most of his books; and although he does not profess to be a Christian, I see biblical principles in his teachings and writings. A lot of what he says boils down to what he calls the three R's of living—

1. Do right.
2. Be real.
3. Take the responsibility.

All through the Scriptures God has laid out those

63

three R's, and the connecting thread always seems to be the word **obedience.**

It takes obedience to what God says to be able to do the right thing, say the right word, and think the right thought. It takes obedience that is willing to risk what "others think" before one can become an honest, genuine person. It also takes obedience and a disciplined commitment to Christ in everyday ethics to be able to confidently assume responsibility for our behavior.

Obedience and discipline, like emotional and physical suffering, are expensive, but they can be the greatest growing forces of our lives.

I have seen some excellent illustrations of obedience and discipline on the part of a few airplane pilots.

For the better part of ten years now my speaking schedule has been very heavy, and because of time pressures, I fly to most out-of-town engagements. I have flown on overseas assignments to the Far East, Middle East, Europe, Central America, and Canada as well as to all the states in America. I've also flown in every type of air vehicle, from big wide-bodied jets, small jets, commuters, single-engine planes to large and small helicopters. Pilots of every description have taken me to my destinations, and many times they have provided me with very colorful, if not downright scary, experiences.

The qualities I like in a pilot, whether he is a captain of a 747 jet or the lone pilot of a single-engine Cessna 150, are obedience and a disciplined mind. I also want him to practice Dr. Glasser's three R's of "doing right, being real, and taking responsibility" in flying.

I'll never forget the time I learned how badly I wanted those qualities in the cockpit. I had to speak in a remote California military base and when a young Christian pilot heard what a time I was having finding a commercial flight, he offered to charter a plane and fly me in.

Without checking his qualifications or his ratings

and licenses (my first mistake), I eagerly jumped at the chance of flying in and out on the same evening.

I met the pilot at the airport and we climbed into the single-engine plane.

I have some fears—like my exaggerated fear of snakes and lizards—but flying is not one of them. However, because I have been flying for so many years I am very familiar with pilot and flying procedures, and I vividly remember a small shiver of fear running down my back when the young man failed to yell "prop clear" as he started the engine, didn't radio the tower for weather, and (scariest of all) did not seem to run through a visible or invisible checklist.

I buckled my seat belt and inquired, "No checklist procedure tonight?"

He smiled. His face was beaming with confidence and he tapped the side of his head as he said, "It's all in here."

"Did you file a flight plan?"

He shook his head no and winked. I wondered what on earth that meant.

There I sat strapped into that Cessna, zooming down the runway beside this bright Christian pilot who had broken every basic rule of flying before the wheels ever left the ground. Outwardly I was a picture of cool calmness, but inside my emotions were having a free-for-all riot.

I've never learned to pilot a plane simply because I love flying as a passenger. But this was one plane trip that made me wish I had taken flying lessons.

The pilot and I skimmed over the foothills and my flight experience warned me that we were entirely too close to the hills.

"Aren't we a little low?" I ventured.

Craning his neck a bit to look over the side he said, "Oh, maybe so. I'll take her up a thousand." Then he added, "If you see anything coming up on your side, let me know."

It was no more than three seconds later when I said,

as controlled as possible, "How do you feel about fire trails coming up from the mountain on my side?" Then I braced myself for the crash landing that I was sure was about to take place.

He took my altitude evaluation in his stride and we climbed another few feet, avoided the crash, and flew on toward our destination.

The rest of the trip was uneventful except that my pilot kept entertaining me with a whole collection of stories about his "near miss" air disasters and landing mishaps.

At one point in his running horror report, he turned to me and said, "You are a very relaxed lady and a marvelous passenger." I smiled and thought, I didn't graduate tops in my class in drama school for nothing!

The trip going home through heavy clouds, fog, and with no radio contact (until I insisted on it), made the earlier flight seem like an effortless exercise.

Silently, I began some diligent conversations with the Lord. I remember bargaining for my life by saying that if the Lord got me down safely, never, ever would I fly with someone who did not have his instrument rating or who was not willing to be **obedient** to air safety rules. The Lord kept His end of the agreement; we landed at 3:00 A.M. in an **out-of-the-way** town because fog had settled over Los Angeles. And since then, by the way, I've kept my part of the bargain!

I want a pilot who is not too big, too important, too experienced, or too seasoned to be obedient. I have learned that when a plane has crashed and the investigators lay the blame on "pilot error," it almost always means a pilot has disobeyed or failed to regard some long-standing, often simple rule.

If obedience to man-made rules and maintaining a disciplined routine are some of the major ways of avoiding physical injury, then obedience to God's rules and laws and keeping a disciplined mind are doubly important to our spiritual health and longevity.

After observing pilots for years, I have come to pray this prayer:

Lord, don't ever let me get so wrapped up in my own goings and comings, my own family, or even my own God-given work that I fail to heed the still, small voice of Your Spirit. Help me to hear You quickly when Your voice is just a whisper so I will not miss the direction of Your plan and end up in devastating disaster.

Abraham and Joshua are often cited as Old Testament examples of obedient servants of God; however, while those men were sterling in their unfailing obedience, I always think of someone else.

I think of Joseph, who would have made a terrific present-day pilot. He was a man of faithful obedience whose disciplined heart and mind never faltered for a moment.

I think we all tend to look admiringly at Joseph, who at the age of thirty was given the powerful job of prime minister by Egypt's Pharaoh. We are so enamored with his success, we gloss over the tumultuous growing up time the Lord allowed Joseph to endure the first thirty years of his life, and we rarely see the strength of Joseph's never-wavering obedience to God.

Read the whole story of Joseph's life in Genesis, chapters 37–50. Once you get started you will find it is one of those hard-to-put-down stories. It presents a clear, unobstructed view of the measure of a man's diligent, dedicated obedience.

Joseph could have become cynical, irreligious, and (especially in Egypt) a sensualist. But circumstances did not mar Joseph's character; rather they strengthened and prepared him for greatness.

We are told of three different occasions when Joseph could have become embittered or could have yielded to a temptation of one kind or another. First, he was sold by his brothers into slavery; then Potiphar's wife tried to seduce him; and finally, he was falsely accused and imprisoned. Yet Joseph remained steadfast and obedient to God.

A lesser man could not have borne these drastic changes of life-styles. Some men could have never gone from home to slavery to dungeons and then, at thirty years of age, to a palace to become one of the greatest men in all of Egypt and second only to the king.

How did Jesus bear his ugly childhood and his later life, which were laced with lies and deception? Joseph endured these traumatic happenings because he understood that **everything** in life has meaning. He knew that even mistakes and misunderstandings have meaning, and so Joseph **chose** to be obedient to God. He coped with the adversities of his life with a moral righteousness and a right state of mind.

He probably did not **feel** obedient after his brothers left him to die down in the pit; nor did he **feel** obedient when he was sold into slavery; and he probably didn't **feel** obedient when he was framed and sent to prison. But obedience was a methodically planned move of his will. He chose obedience.

In respect for his obedience, God gave Joseph the sensitivity to see the proper priority of prisons and palaces; and so, in return for Joseph's unfailing obedience, the Lord gave him immense security amidst all the changes of his life. The Scripture says, "The Lord was with Joseph." (Gen. 39:21, KJV).

Joseph disciplined his mind with strict obedience and learned the lessons of the soul. By obeying God he learned how to rule; and when the great moment came, Joseph stepped from prison into the most prominent position a ruler could have—and he was already seasoned and highly skilled for the challenge.

Had Joseph remained at home, a favorite son of his father, or returned there at some point in time or had Potiphar not thrown him into prison, he would not have become the prime minister of Egypt. But Joseph's whole life was one of obedience. It started with his obeying God first—then his father, employer, jailer, and eventually the king of Egypt.

Joseph was obedient during setbacks, delays, and even while sitting on the sidelines watching someone else carry the ball. He understood that God's delays are a part of our spiritual education, for in waiting we learn to develop our faith and trust. Joseph knew, too, that to accept the circumstances God sends, though their usefulness or purpose is not understood, is true obedience and submission to the will of God.

Had Joseph not chosen to be an obedient son of God, he never would have been the deliverer of the Egyptian people nor of his own family; nor could he have been the instrument and channel to fulfill God's promise and purpose.

Like Joseph, most of us desire some form of power, talents, usefulness, or blessings in this life; but what we need is a measure of Joseph's concept of unfailing obedience and untiring discipline to sustain us in the midst of overwhelming adversities and puzzling, frustrating events.

Just this year in my own life, I have tripped over the word obedience several times, and lately I've been running smack into the "obedience" wall.

I can hear Jim Dobson saying, "The Lord says, 'This is what I want you to do, now you do it.' " But not too long ago my level of disciplined obedience seemed to be running low.

At the first of this year, my jaw pain was acting up more than usual. If the Lord wasn't going to heal it just now, I felt I should give up all singing and public speaking. The price was too high—speaking and having it followed by such acute pain was simply not worth it.

I could hear the Lord's veto, but it was only whispered, and so I ignored it.

About the time I thought I had definitely reached a decision not to take any more engagements, I had to fulfill a long-standing booking at Robert Schuller's church in Garden Grove, California. I reluctantly went, and from the first four bars of my beginning song and on into my talk and the luncheon that followed, my jaw and entire head pounded into an explosion of pain.

Even as I spoke I mentally said, "This is it! I'm not going to go on taking this pain."

The still, small voice said, "This is what I want you

to do—now do it." I closed my ears and finished speaking—grateful that it was over.

When I sat down, Jeenie, one of my secretaries, handed me a note. It was from a dear lady wanting to know if we would like to meet Corrie ten Boom. I scribbled back that yes I would, if it was not an imposition. But privately I wondered if I could endure the pain long enough to even see Corrie—much less meet and converse with her.

After the luncheon, with my head still violently throbbing, we went to meet that beautiful Dutch saint.

I must say that I didn't go see Corrie ten Boom that warm, spring afternoon in order to grow by the method of obedience. I simply went with my secretary and her friend to meet and enjoy Corrie. How differently it all worked out.

When I entered Corrie's room, she was lying in bed, all propped up by pillows and wearing a frilly eyelet-edged pink and blue housecoat.

"I'm not sick—just resting," the eighty-four-year-old beauty hastened to assure me.

Her shining white hair formed a literal halo around her face. The pink in her cheeks was the exact shade of pink in her housecoat, and her blue eyes danced a continuous jig of joy. Even though pain was blurring my vision, I remember thinking that I had never seen anyone so incredibly beautiful, nor had I been so close and within touching range of Jesus as I was then.

Corrie's presence in that room would have been a heady experience in itself, but the presence of Jesus was a little more than overwhelming. She motioned for us to sit down, but I felt like Moses must have felt before the Lord on holy ground and I wished I could remove my shoes. However, when I remembered the small hole my toenail had made in my hose, I compromised and did the next best thing—I remained standing.

"Joyce, why are you standing?" she asked. I was afraid she wouldn't buy my Moses-on-holy-ground theory, and so I mumbled something about not wanting to tire her. I was graciously told to sit down.

I did.

We talked of many things.

Years ago Corrie had spoken at my father's church in Reseda, California, just a few months before my mother died. Corrie's long-standing acquaintanceship with the ways of dying caused her to clearly see death's shadow hovering over my mother, and in their first moment of meeting, Corrie said to my mother, "Oh, I see you are going to heaven soon."

My sister tells me that my mother nodded yes and Corrie continued, "When you see Betsy and Father, tell them I said hello and that I send my love."

I'm sure my mother kept her promise a few months later, and I had always wanted to thank Corrie for the gentle way she encouraged my mother's walk across the bridge of death.

That afternoon, too, we talked of Corrie's newest books, of her little tape recorder laying by her pillow; and then, in a way not known or practiced by many Christian celebrities, she straightened up, looked directly at me and said, "Now, that's enough about me. Tell me about Joyce Landorf and your books."

I was deeply touched by her lack of self-centeredness and her genuine interest in someone else. My pain was numbing my ability to speak very well, but I managed to tell her of my teen-age rebellion to God and the church, my mother's prayers, my disastrous marriage to Dick, our suicide attempts, and finally, our conversion and our life now in Christ.

Corrie shook her head, leaned forward in her bed, and said with a bright enthusiasm, "Just think, Joyce, your mother's prayers are still being answered now—years after her death—and God is really using you!"

It might have been right then, or just a little later, but suddenly I could not hear Corrie or the voices of those around me—only the still, small voice of the Lord, which by this time was through with whispering.

And I clearly heard, "Corrie endured months in various prisons, and years at Hitler's Ravensbruck concentration camp, yet she was obedient to Me. Joyce, **what is a jaw ache?**" I had to answer, "Nothing, Lord, compared to that."

And I went home crying and saying, "Yes, Lord. I'll continue. I may not be able to sing as many songs or speak at as many places, but I will **continue to obey you** and I will not count the cost as exorbitant but appropriate."

Aristotle said, "Wicked men obey from fear, good men from love."

The kind of obedience God wants from us should not be motivated out of a frightened or intimidated spirit, but out of our love.

Jesus Himself called us to obedience: "If you **love** me, obey me" (John 14:15, TLB, emphasis mine).

When Moses was explaining to the Israelites the importance of keeping God's commandments, he promised, "If you obey them they will give you a reputation for wisdom and intelligence" (Deut. 4:6, TLB). Then, in order to encourage them to **continue** in obedience, he instructed the men to "Be very careful never to forget what you have seen God doing for you. May his miracles have a deep and permanent effect upon your lives! Tell your children and your grandchildren about the glorious miracles he did" (Deut. 4:9, TLB).

Since Dick and I have just recently become grandparents, this verse has taken on a new glow; and even though our little grandbaby, April Joy, is only eight months old, I caught her grandpa whispering in her ear the other day about how good God is and how He's blessed her.

Moses, a real and practical man, knew there would be terribly hard days and times of deep affliction for his people, but majestically he added this glorious promise—a promise given in reward for obedience:

When thou art in tribulation, and all these things are come upon thee, even in the latter days, if thou turn to the Lord thy God, and shalt be obedient unto his voice; (For the Lord thy God is a merciful God;) He will not forsake thee, neither destroy thee, nor forget the covenant of thy fathers which he sware unto them (Deut. 4:30, 31, KJV).

So our obedience is rewarded by God, and this verse tells us God will not forsake, destroy, or forget us, in our daily growing process, if we practice obedient living.

Clearly I can hear, "This is what I want you to do—now you do it."

And I have to answer, "Yes, Lord."

Chapter Five

Growing Through Belonging

In the triangle of love between ourselves,
God, and other people is found the secret
of existence and the best foretaste, I
suspect, that we can have on earth of what
heaven will probably be like.

—Samuel M. Shoemaker

We exist and live in a society that plunges headlong into the race to **belong.** We want desperately to be accepted, we want to belong. We buy memberships into everything from tennis and country clubs to discount and wholesale stores. Yet, when it comes to belonging to the body of Christ, there are still many people and groups of people who insist on going it alone like some kind of Christian lone ranger.

I have looked into more than a few tanned, windburned teen-age faces and heard words like these: "I can worship God on my surfboard a lot better than in some stuffy traditional church."

Equally as many times I have met people who attend a "closed" church.

I remember once talking with a dedicated Christian businessman who was seated next to me on a plane. He poured out his troubled heart in regard to his terrible uneasiness over the lack of vision in his church. While he loved the people and the pastor, his main question to me was: "Do you think God is leading me out of such a church?"

The membership of the church was limited to about fifty people who had no outreach program to non-

Christians in the community. The meetings were three to four hours long, with lots of good congregational singing. The sermons did not vary or change in topics or words over the years. The church's social life consisted of a midweek dinner and other than that the members were not encouraged to be friends with any outsider or to go anywhere else.

There was never any special meeting for the youth; nor was there any summer program for children such as daily vacation Bible school. When I asked what the budget was for home and foreign missions, the man shook his head sadly and said, "We have no missionary budget or outreach whatsoever."

In his words, his whole church-life experience boiled down to "getting together to get a blessing."

The surfer with his I'll-do-it-my-own-way spirit and the businessman who belongs to a church with restricted tunnel vision are at opposite ends of the poles in their methods, but both are missing the same thing— God's most unique method of teaching us to become giants in a land of spiritual and moral dwarfs.

We grow corporately. A great church **can** be an avenue to our learning and it **can** lead us into living stable, unshakeable lives if we recognize its potential and seek the church of God's choice for us.

Paul wrote to the church in Corinth about their joining together to be members of one body and at one point said: "Now here is what I am trying to say: All of you together are the one body of Christ and each one of you is a separate and necessary part of it" (1 Cor. 12:27, TLB).

To the Ephesians, Paul said we "belong in God's household with every other Christian" (Eph. 2:19, TLB). Paul never described the process of being a Christian as a game played unilaterally. He always referred to this process as a thing we do **together** via teamwork.

To the surfer, I would have to admit that worshiping God in nature's beautiful seascape of waves and foam can be done, at least to some degree, but God's creation of all nature is only one small dimension of God's creativity. Our God is not limited to creating lovely beaches, mountains, and other majestic scenic beauties. He has many other sides and His abilities are like hundreds of lights refracted into a thousand different angles. To see God in only one area, the area of His material creations, is to miss the magnificent wholeness of God.

Our God is not only the Creator of all life, but He is our Sovereign King, our Savior, Shepherd, and the God of forgiveness, mercy, and salvation. You don't quite get all that shooting curls on a surfboard or relaxing on sun-drenched beaches. Besides, the surfer out there on his board is ignoring a very important principle—that of belonging to a group of believers.

The Scriptures tell us not to forsake the assembling of ourselves together and for good reason. We need collective fellowship, comfort, and encouragement.

Even a surfer gets off his board at one time or another, and as he relaxes on the beach, guess what he does? He talks with other surfers about their mutual passion for surfing until they all return to the water to surf. As with any group of like-minded people, it's called "collective fellowship." People really do need people.

Paul wrote, "We who believe are carefully joined together with Christ as parts of a beautiful, constantly growing temple for God" (Eph. 2:21, TLB).

To think we can grow, blossom, and bloom separately is not only ridiculous but highly frustrating in this stress-and-trauma-filled world.

I'm sure this is why Paul encouraged us to "talk with each other **much** about the Lord, quoting psalms and hymns and singing sacred songs, making music in your hearts to the Lord" (Eph. 5:19, TLB, emphasis mine). He knew we would need all the loving encouragement of belonging that we could get.

77

My strongest words to the surfer would be just this: whenever a believer habitually or by principle removes himself from belonging to a body of other believers, he ends up a defeated, often bitter loser.

I personally know men and women who became disillusioned with "belonging to the body of believers," and for one reason or another left the church. They went off to do their own thing and said, "I'll worship God in my own way"; or they used the tired old cliché, "I believe in God—in here," as they thumped their chests with a smug pride or winked their eyes with a look of secret wisdom.

As I have watched their lives over the years, all I have seen is the ignorance of their decision and the brokenness that is reflected in the lives of their entire family.

Henry Ward Beecher once said, "The church is not a gallery for the exhibition of eminent Christians, but a school for the education of imperfect ones."

What better place can we learn about
    the kind of love that comes from really caring,
    the freedom from guilt that comes with God's
        forgiveness,
    the joys of giving that come with stewardship, or
    the unsurpassed empathy and comfort that come
        out of hearts eager to please God?

What better arena for real lessons than in a godly church?

The church, when led by the Holy Spirit and full of believers who are committed to the "triangle of love" among ourselves, God, and all others in the world today, is a healthy, beautifully growing body—a real place of learning.

To the businessman and other people who belong to a "closed church," I would have to concede that drawing together in a tight, elite circle of like minds, praising God, singing hymns, and taking no responsibility for any sinner outside would probably produce a euphoric sense of well-being and spiritual security. However, one of the greatest dangers would be the formation of a thick cloud of spiritual pride that would blind their eyes to the need for inner growth and certainly to the need for taking action on Jesus' Great Commission.

The writer of Acts quoted Jesus as saying, "But when the Holy Spirit has come upon you, you will receive power to testify about me with great effect, to the people in Jerusalem, throughout Judea, in Samaria, and to the ends of the earth, about my death and resurrection" (Acts 1:8, TLB).

So to stay safely locked into a closed church means that the Good News will never reach the sidewalk in front of the church much less the town around it. The cloistered closed church violates our commitment to Spirit-led witnessing, and our growing potential reaches its saturation point very quickly. Spiritually, we die off right in the pew.

Isolated monasteries and convents never really caught on because the men and women who retreated there tried to get **out** of this world rather than **into** it as Christ commanded.

If it is true that we grow through belonging to a Christ-centered church, one that reaches out to the surrounding community and world, then it is equally true that we need Christian friends.

Again, we grow corporately.

Psalm 1:1 tells us that a man is blessed who does not walk in the counsel of the ungodly. That verse implies that when we need advice and counsel, we should seek it only from godly people.

If we have to live this life, which at times can be pretty gruesome, God has given us several ways to endure, and certainly one of them is the valued love and advice of a godly friend.

The Scriptures are full of admonishments for us to be a friend and to make friends. Joseph Joubert said, "If we spend our lives loving, we will have no leisure to complain or feel unhappiness."

It seems that the first Christians spent a good deal of time learning how to love each other and become

79

friends. Romans 12:10 tells us about "brotherly love"; Galatians 2:9 talks of the "right hands of fellowship"; Hebrews 13:1, of brotherly love again; and 1 John 4:20, 21 really comes down hard on the importance of loving our brothers. It says,

> If anyone says "I love God," but keeps on hating his brother, he is a liar; for if he doesn't love his brother who is right there in front of him, how can he love God whom he has never seen? And God himself has said that one must love not only God, but his brother too (1 John 4:20,21, TLB).

I have recently developed a new perspective on this business of growing through belonging and cultivating Christian friends. When I did the research for my biblical novel about Martha, **I Came to Love You Late,** I was fascinated by the types of people who were drawn to Jesus. I found that whole groups of people were drawn to Him by His magnetic charisma. He was always accompanied by smaller groups of believing followers, His dedicated disciples, and those disciples who chose to be especially close to Him. But the Bible records Jesus as having three special friends: Martha, Mary, and Lazarus.

It was to his friends' houses that Jesus came to rest, eat, and at times retreat. I find it interesting that Jesus, the Son of God, needed human companionship. He made regular visits to their homes, ate and conversed with them, and as the Scriptures tell us, He dearly loved these friends.

Was Jesus not, in fact, setting down a living example of a principle and commandment He had taught publicly? The commandment to love one another is the beginning of growing together through belonging, and if Jesus Himself needed to belong, how much more must we?

The verse in John where Jesus gives us the commandment to love one another is followed immediately by a very interesting statement. Jesus says, "Your strong love for each other will prove to the world that you are my disciples" (John 13:35, TLB).

My dear friend Keith Korstjens was talking about the marital problems he deals with each day as a counselor and pastor, and at one point in his conversation he said, "You know, Joyce, the more I talk and counsel with people, the more I am convinced that in every relationship we either **actively create love** or we **actively destroy love.**"

The Christian has a choice again. He can create or destroy love in any relationship. If he chooses to **create** loving bonds, then he is giving the world the best proof of his Christianity. He must reach out, embrace others, and **create** friendships.

Not only does growing through belonging happen by our attending a Spirit-led church and cultivating friends, but it also happens through discipleship. There are two areas, or rather time frames, when we need the fine tuning of discipling.

The first time for discipling, that is, being a teachable student, comes right after our conversion to Christ.

We need to continue on with the parent, pastor, or person who introduced us to Christ and who is our spiritual father or mother. I cannot stress too much the value of staying and learning from those who are more spiritually mature. We need their spiritual "shepherdship" and guidance until we are ready to move from the milk stage of babyhood into the meaty sessions of adulthood.

When Dick and I became Christians, no one actually helped us in a step-by-step fashion to accept Christ. Many people had prayed for us, but we were alone and separated from human contact when we invited Christ into our lives. However, the need for discipling was very great and God placed us rather quickly in the right church and Dr. Ted Cole, our pastor, became our teacher and discipler. Both Dick and I took notes on each sermon or Sunday school class our pastor taught, and we continued that procedure for over three exciting "baby Christian" years.

Pete Gillquist was led to the Lord years ago by Ray Nethery, and in Pete's words, "As I look back, had I not relied heavily on Ray Nethery's wisdom and insight to help guide my decisions in life, no telling where I'd be." Both Dick and I can say that same thing about our pastor's wisdom and viable Christ-centered discipling.

John Randolph once wrote,

> I believe I should have been swept away by the flood of French infidelity, if it had not been for one thing: the remembrance of the time when my sainted mother used to make me kneel by her side, taking my little hands in hers, and caused me to repeat the Lord's Prayer.

His mother's first efforts in discipling her son left their marks, and John Randolph grew into godly manhood.

The second time frame for lessons on discipleship comes during our continued daily process as a **maturing** Christian. I said "maturing"—not "matured"—because I believe the process is never ending. Even people such as the sainted Corrie ten Boom, believe it or not, are still in the process of maturing, ripening, and becoming God's people.

When I asked Pete Gillquist how he grows spiritually, now that he's a maturing Christian, he answered, "I grow because of four times a year." Then he explained that four times a year he gets together with six Spirit-led friends for a week at a time to pray, share, encourage, debate, and even correct each other. They put themselves under the authority of God and each other, and the lovely, yet strenuous work of discipling goes on—hot and heavy, but productive!

We all need that friend or set of friends who can critique our Christian efforts from a **loving** perspective. I hasten to say though that I don't know **anyone** who can take flat-out criticism, even when it's disguised by the thin veil of "I tell you this in Christian love." But all of us need a timely critique, an update, or a course correction from time to time. It seems to me that one of the most ideal and practical ways of changing our direction or of keeping on God's right-on course is Pete's four-times-a-year plan.

It will not be easy to find the people, place, or time to put yourself into such a plan; but, if you want to badly enough, you can find people and places, and you will take or make time.

Years ago I circled all the "I wills" in several Psalms, and I read one in Psalm 119 just yesterday. David said, "I will"; he made up his mind. I doubt the "I will" decision was a snap one or easily done.

I wanted to put this principle of reevaluation into practice, and so I've just arranged to spend a few days with my friend Clare Bauer. I will be tired from my speaking engagements in Michigan, but I'm going to take all those crazy flights to Idaho before coming back to my home in California anyway. Clare and I both need the lovely work of discipling that God always seems to do in our lives when we are together.

One last thing growing through belonging gives us is a new feeling of togetherness brought on by a united effort. I am particularly aware of this in the lives of Christian women everywhere I go.

Perhaps this has happened significantly in the last five years because of the enormous pressure brought about by women's lib groups. Today's woman is hearing a thousand different drum beats that tell her who she is supposed to be, what she is supposed to feel, and how she is supposed to succeed.

At first, I think Christian women panicked and for good reason. It seemed the main message of the women's movement was: "You're dumb if you are satisfied with being a wife, mother, and homemaker." From every form of media available, the Christian woman got the impression that everyone was in step but her. Little by little, however, Christian women began seeking out other Christian women, and the bonds of Christian love began to strengthen.

I get quite annoyed when the women's liberation spokespersons say they speak for all women. They don't speak for me, nor do they speak for thousands of Christian women all over the world. But for awhile we were all intimidated into thinking that to be a Christian woman meant being very elderly, very weird, very much a malcontent who needs a crutch, or a combination of all three.

But our panic was short-lived because, little by little, Christian women began seeking out other Christian women, and they began banding together in many different ways and in all sorts of areas.

They came together in the traditional ways of
* Bible study groups,
* prayer groups, and
* koinonia groups.

They also began to gather at public functions like
* day-long family seminars,
* weekend retreats for women, and
* weekly classes on inner and outer Christian beauty.

But most amazing of all is the way thousands of Christian women have united together in a quiet, rather private way like
* two neighborhood women who share Christ over coffee,
* six to twelve women who pray together in a prayer chain (I have twelve of the most precious from our church who pray regularly for me in a prayer chain. I call them the "all-the-difference-in-the-world bunch" because that's exactly how my schedule and ministry have improved since they have been my prayer partners this year), and
* individual women who are reading not only their Bibles but also the tremendous Christian books on the market today.

In all of this, the Christian women around the world are the fastest growing group of people I know.

My brother-in-law and sister are pastoring a church in Michigan. Here is part of a letter from one of the great Christian gals in that church. She has a lot to say about growing through belonging.

I'm a member of Central Wesleyan where Pastor Paul and Marilyn are ministering to us beautifully. I love them very much already.

Lately I'm learning more and more what it really means to be part of God's family together, and parts of His body.

Because I've read your books, and now because I know of you through Paul and Marilyn, I'm prompted to write.

I'm becoming more and more aware of the beautiful, God-gifted people around me, and I am learning to recognize and appreciate them as such. I appreciate your ministry through your books, music, and speaking ability because I see Christ fulfilling Himself through you—your talents and skills—and I am seeing the "beauty of Jesus" in you, with grace and charm the world doesn't show. I just wanted you to know I'm thankful for you today.

Then, also, because I know you are struggling with a physical problem, I'm praying for you. I recognize that it's my "responsibility and privilege" to pray for you, as my sister in Christ, which brings peace of heart and a thankful spirit according to Colossians 3:15.

Today, I pray that the Holy Spirit will encourage and love you in a way that you'll experience the joy of our Lord.

In Christian love,
Phyl

She names three definite areas of growth:

(1) learning what it means to be a part of God's family,

(2) becoming aware of others and recognizing and appreciating them, and

(3) realizing her responsibilities as a Christian woman.

How beautifully she is growing. Yet, she is only one of thousands of Christian women who are learning the joys of belonging to God's family.

There are many alert and bright-eyed women who are taking the baton of the relay race of life and running to win! Enjoy Paul's words, even though he wrote them so long ago: "Now you are no longer strangers to God and foreigners to heaven, but you are members of God's very own family, citizens of God's country, and you **belong** in God's household with every other Christian" (Eph. 2:19, TLB, emphasis mine).

Chapter Six

Growing Through the Three D's

God asks no man whether he will accept life.
That is not the choice.
You must take it.
The only choice is **How.**

—Henry Ward Beecher

I can think of three words, all beginning with the letter "d" that describe potential sources of growing. I say "potential sources of growing" because often we refuse to accept these sources as ways for God to mold our lives and to cause us to mature.

The first "d" word is "differences." Believe it or not, we can grow through our differences. We need not be horrified that somebody butters his toast, parks his car, or combs his hair differently from us. We need not be "grieved in our spirits" because so-and-so has deliberately chosen a spiritual position that is not up to our prescribed image. In fact, those differences may be the very way God leads us into acceptance and tolerance.

Each time I hear one Christian criticizing or judging another Christian's spiritual progress, his church affiliation, or his denominational practices, I am reminded of a rather simple yet clear analogy.

Not five minutes from my home is a large and beautiful shopping center. It is an enclosed mall arrangement, surrounded by acres of parking lots, and it boasts of over two hundred fine, quality stores. With excellent management and maintenance, lots of foot traffic, and artistically planned indoor landscaping, the center is enjoying a very profitable operation.

I do not think all two hundred stores are "super" or "fantastic" as their ads indicate; in fact, I don't shop in a lot of them. Yet nothing but lack of time stops me from being one of the center's best customers.

Just yesterday, I added up all the dress shops, on one of the large directory boards. Not counting four large major department stores, there were fifty specialty shops that sell women's clothes exclusively.

Although all these stores offer women's garments, each caters to a particular age group, size, type, or style. Out of fifty stores, I'm interested in shopping in only five or six. My twenty-two-year-old daughter Laurie, who kids me about the fact that she wouldn't be caught dead in one of those "older-lady shops," buys her clothes in five or six different stores.

But we both go to the center and have a marvelous time together. We shop or browse and neither of us thinks it is "just awful" about those other forty or so stores whose doors we never darken.

Also, we would never dream of going into those unpatronized stores to seek out the managers or some saleslady, and "in love" tell them how far wrong their buyer has gone or how they should spruce up their store or merchandise.

But Christians are super serious about their differences. This was abruptly pointed out once when a friend of mine gave me a very hard time over the church we attend. I asked him, "Why can't you accept me as a born-again child of God, just as I have accepted you—as a believer?"

He got very agitated and shouted, "Because Jesus is coming back again very soon, and you and everybody in THAT church are going to hell, that's why!"

I am deeply saddened by the lack of love and unity between believers and by remarks like this one from my well-meaning friend. When are we going to stop shooting our poison arrows into other Christians who are firm and solid in their faith, but who do not cross their t's and dot their i's in our specifically prescribed ways?

There seems to be some kind of holy crusade going on between so many Christians. The hot or cold wars are rather endless—

- between excited, enthusiastic charismatics and dyed-in-the-wool, stanch noncharismatics.
- between sprinkled Presbyterians, immersed Baptists, and those who believe water baptism is essential for salvation.
- between rigidly proud "straight" people and deliberately "loose" counterculture groups.
- between left- and right-wing believers, and even between those who embrace the Bible's new translations (including paraphrased versions) and those who read **only** King James.

We Christians may not see eye to eye on these and other issues in the church, but certainly, in the name of common sense and Christian maturity, we should be able to walk in unity without waging war on one another.

In his profoundly great and disturbing book **Let's Quit Fighting About the Holy Spirit,** Pete Gillquist tells of a delightful fantasy conversation between two men who lived in Jesus' day and who were both healed of blindness. As the story goes, two men got to comparing notes one day about their healings and they discovered Jesus was the healer in both cases.

Next, they discussed the method and technique of Jesus' healing and to their dismay, they discovered that Jesus used an instant-type procedure to heal one; but with the other, He used a totally different mud-on-the-eyes approach.

Both men were frustrated, but positive of one thing: Jesus could not possibly have used the "other" method to heal. In great disbelief, one man said to the other man, "There's no way it could have happened like

89

that!" And then Pete's punch line follows: "And there you have it, folks. The start of the world's first two denominations. The Mudites and the Anti-Mudites."

Some of us are terribly busy being in one camp or the other. We have long since forgotten that the Scriptures call us over and over again to a ministry of love. But mostly we have forgotten that mature growing Christians make allowances for each other, forbear one another in love, and remain loyal at all costs.

In the fourth chapter of Ephesians, Paul practically begged the Christians of Ephesus to act and walk in a manner that would be appropriate to their calling. Then he wrote, "Be humble and gentle. Be patient with each other, making allowance for each other's faults because of your love" (Eph. 4:2, TLB). The King James Version reads, ". . . forbearing one another in love."

In other words, there are many splendid opportunities in our relationships with other Christians when we should simply shut up, put up, forbear, or make allowances because of our love! My secretary Brenda made this comment when she read this book in its rough draft form: "Why does there have to be so much competition? We're all on the same team!" It is our Christian responsibility to stop making a federal case out of our nit-picking differences, and to allow God to teach us some sober maturity.

Your worship service may be conducted in a totally different way from mine, your theology and life-style may differ considerably from mine, and your goals or priorities may be worlds apart from mine; but both of us had better remember that the only unpardonable sin in heaven or on earth is rejecting Jesus as Lord and Savior.

One difference that rankles and repulses Christian men and women the most in our society today is the ancient sin of homosexuality. There's nothing new about homosexuality—it existed in ancient Greece and Rome—and Paul, bless his courageous heart, dealt with it when he was on earth.

I suspect with today's emphasis on "coming out of the closet" and "doing your own thing," we will tend to think that sexual sin is more widespread today, and that there are more sexual deviates than in years past. Actually, we are simply **hearing** more about it. It's been here a long time.

Since even the psychiatrists and psychology experts are divided on causes and treatment for the homosexual, I was thrilled this year to see the Melodyland Church in Anaheim, California, add EXIT (Ex-gay Intervention Team) to its Hot Line Center. Their program is headed by two former homosexuals, and their work is being uniquely blessed of God. They work from the premise that homosexuality is a sin, but that God can deliver a person from it. The center helps the homosexual live a straight but abundant life in Christ, and it gives its prayerful support to new men and women in Christ much like Alcoholics Anonymous does for the alcoholic.

To most of us though, we are too repulsed by the sin to show any compassion or to lovingly deal with the homosexual. We seem to be far better at accepting those who have committed violent crimes, even to the point of supporting a prison chaplain ministry, than we are at accepting the homosexual sinner.

I am deeply convicted about my own attitudes, especially when I read about the way Jesus handled the prostitute, the adulterer, and even the common thief on the cross. He did not pull Himself away from sinners in a don't-touch-me-because-you-are-unclean gesture; He did not get angry and shake them by their garments; He did not hold them up as examples of sin for the world to see; nor did He say, "How could you **do** such a thing?"

Never, not even once, did He put down the sinner with verbal condemnation. But in each case the sinner knew the extent, depth, and seriousness of his own sin and in repentance, experienced the loving forgiveness of God Himself.

I will never be a lesbian—just as I will never be a

murderer—for these are not my sins. However, I must never forget that I am a sinner saved by God's grace. How dare any of us condemn or criticize the sin of others or hold ourselves up as paragons of virtue when we feel we've been rescued from the sea of sin and now sit safely in our little boats of forgiveness.

My straight life is vastly different from a gay life, but I pray God develops in me a real and honest love toward those who are most different from me; in fact, I want the kind of love that Christ showed to broken people around Him when He was here.

We will never mature in Christ if we spend our energies and time preaching **against** sinners. We must give our efforts to **lovingly dealing** with the sin and get on to the business of healing.

I am aware that some of you may violently disagree with what I have just written, but I pray that you ask God to make the last several paragraphs a time of learning or a time of examining your own soul.

But that's the problem with differences—sometimes they grow too big to overcome.

Last week I got a red hot letter from a Christian lady who took real issue with me for something I had written in my column for the "Power for Living" Sunday school paper. She definitely did not agree with me and so she wrote a long letter filled with Scripture to back up her claims about how wrong, wrong, wrong I was.

I answered her in the only way possible: "Isn't it wonderful that in Christ we have the lovely freedom to disagree?"

Most of us need to learn that we can be brothers and sisters in Christ without being identical twins.

It is uniquely true, and only true of real Christians, that there is a unity through diversity. It is possible through Christ!

The second "d" word can be used as mightily as the first one. It is "daily." Did you know we can grow from current events and daily newspapers, magazines and, even from the six o'clock news? It's true, but most Christians do not want to use this means for growth because if something in the news media really reaches us it usually stirs up concern and we are motivated into **acting** or **doing** something.

This seems to be true even when we are talking about Christian periodicals, magazines, and media efforts. For instance, the **Los Angeles Times** ran a story that said that a Christian newspaper had suspended its publication after two million dollars had been invested in it. The publisher issued a statement in the final edition explaining: "Many Christians are not really interested in keeping up with the news events affecting Christian life, church, and society. There seems to be an avoidance of knowing, probably because knowing challenges us to do—and many of us are not ready for that challenge."*

We like staying away from daily challenges, yet the New Testament tells us to be good, obedient citizens—yes, even to paying our dues to the tax collector. From a biblical standpoint, our conduct in the community around us should be one of alertness, sensitivity, and responsibility. Christians who demean and criticize the media, the newspapers, and the news magazines become isolationists who shut off growth and challenges and simply stagnate in their own apathetic pool of indifference.

Once when I was speaking at a writers' conference, the small group of would-be authors were asked what in their lives contributed the most to their writing abilities, or what was the main source of inspiration for their writing.

Several writers shared, and their answers involved everything from God's direct words and inspiration, or some tragic or painful incident, to the inspiration and education given by a gifted Christian teacher or a godly mother or father.

Then one woman stood and said that her inspiration

*Los Angeles Times, Sept. 3, 1977.

came from reading and looking at **nothing** but the Bible. She went on to say that she did not watch or own a television set; she did not subscribe to a newspaper or any secular or Christian magazine; nor did she read any books because most of that "stuff," she said, was "ungodly and unnecessary." Her voice swelled with pride as she related how many hours a day she read the Bible and how awful newspapers were and how sinful it was to watch television.

I don't know what's happened to the lady in the years since that conference, but I do know she has missed out on the viable world around her and in doing so has never felt the thrill of challenges nor seen the power of God at work here on this earth. I imagine that her writing will be a bit irrelevant.

How can we ever open up our hearts to love, minister, and witness in the small corner of the world we live in if we refuse to open our ears to the crying around us and our minds and hearts to people's needs?

I believe one way to enlarge our capacity for caring and learning is by reading the daily and weekly accounts of the society, community, and world around us.

The newspapers, magazines, and six o'clock news put us in touch with the reality of life. We may not like what we find out; we may find it extremely disagreeable, even sinful, but the media can bring people and their needs to our attention. Someone once said the church is not a hotel for saints but a hospital for sinners, and so it is with Christians. We are not left on earth to relax and collect unemployment but to work, seeing to the spiritual and physical needs of the world around us. We are told to work, for the night is coming; yet some of us have been so cooped up in our own little houses that we are blissfully unaware of the approaching evening shadows or the broken lives on our block. The newspaper and media can put this into a realistic focus for us, and quite quickly.

I read the **Los Angeles Times** each day in addition to my Bible and two devotional books. I see that paper as one giant Wednesday night prayer request sheet!

Look at my newspaper today. On page 1, the right-hand column lead story seems to indicate that our President is going to need a super-human amount of wisdom if he is to handle this week's White House crisis. The press is saying, "The President's honeymoon with the country is definitely over," and so this man—the highest governing person in the United States—needs as much prayer support from Christians as he can possibly get.

On the second page is a story about a young man reared in a strong, loving Catholic family who grew up to depart from his parents' training and to eventually become a spy for some other country. Now he is sentenced to forty years in prison, and he and his family are devastated by this. I don't know them, but from all the article says of the boy and his family, they must be in deep shock. It is safe to assume that at some point in time they will desperately try to figure out just where their faith failed them, or how God fits into all of this, or how they will survive the loss and humiliation. They must be floundering in their sea of questions even while I read this account, and so I stop and ask the Lord to somehow lead them and mend their shattered souls and fragmented dreams.

On page 4 is an interesting story that tells about seventeen hundred people in the Russian city of Gorki who signed a petition asking the government to reopen one of the city's closed churches. The article goes on to say that ten years ago a similar petition drive met with threats and reprisals from the authorities. Nine of the most active participants lost their jobs and one leader was threatened with incarceration in a mental asylum. My gut-level feeling tells me these Russian citizens are my brothers and sisters and I need to hold them dearly and lovingly before the Lord today.

On page 17 is the story of famine and disease in the Mideast. It helps me respect the stew that's simmering on my stove, and my thank-you prayer at the table is not memorized and glibly mouthed but genuine.

The sports section, which I barely skim, reminds

me afresh that my sports-fan husband is out of town on a business trip and is working on a tough assignment. I stop and pray for the needy sports fans he works with and ask God to give him "journeying mercies."

The women's section has a large feature story, spread across the top half of the paper on a leading women's rights leader. The glowing article tells about all the triumphs of this year's resolutions and achievements. The piece, covering more space than the paper would ever allow for a report on a Christian convention or seminar, is accompanied by a big picture of the activist/editor/speaker who is shown smiling and raising her clenched fist.

The whole report challenged me, broke my heart, and made me dedicate myself anew to ministering to women. The women's movement pictured on the women's page today alerts me that it's time we of the silent majority spoke up to say: we will not be put down because of our faith or slandered because of the biblical principles we live by. We will be, to the best of our abilities, the women God wants us to be. To be those women mean experiencing the true meaning of freedom and joy!

The theater and TV section, with its sensational movie captions and its descriptions of television shows, which must come across like drawn-out dirty jokes, was a marvelous contrast to the Bible and the books **Knowing God** and **A Touch of Wonder** I am reading each morning.

I put the paper down, thankful and rejoicing that I belong to the Lord Jesus Christ and His church instead of to the world. I also know and understand the world around me a little better; and while much of what I read was discouraging and painted dark pictures, above the sound of the world's drums, I could hear the steady beating of God's voice saying,

> Be still and know I am God—
> Be not afraid—
> I will never leave you—

Will you take the Great Commission?
Will you feed my sheep?
Do you care?

Once more my daily newspaper shoved and pushed me into praying and caring and, above all, into growing.

Before I leave the discussion of the word **daily,** I want to write about one other aspect of the word. I am quite sure that just as God teaches us through the big important issues and crises of life, He also is perfectly capable of teaching us through daily little episodes which—while they are not earthshaking—do tend to set our teeth on edge. I'm talking about our growing through little things daily.

Let me illustrate by using a part of a letter from a friend of mine. He writes,

The other night I got a call from a brother in our church whose plumbing had just burst in the ceiling of his two-year-old home, ruining ceilings in three rooms along with carpet, padding and walls in those areas. Damage soared into the hundreds of dollars.

After the cleanup operations were complete I said to him, "Buddy, how are you holding up under all this? Are you still on top of it with the Lord?"

His reply was a classic: "Yeah, I can handle the big things with the Lord. For some reason they're the easy ones to give thanks for. My problem is some of the little things which happen which bug me to death. Often those are the tough things to let go."

The same is often true with me. I got cheated out of thousands of bucks on a crooked "Christian" land deal and was able to turn it over to the Lord instantly. But, on the other hand, I'll go through the supermarket line and get ripped off for 29 cents when the gal fails to honor a coupon, and when I get home and realize the mistake I sometimes find myself sulking for an hour or two.

My friend's true-to-life exposé is so typical and so normal that it is almost humorous. How often have we seen the same thing happen in our own homes?

I remember before Dick and I were born-again people, our ten-month-old daughter Laurie had a sinus infection that put her on the hospital's critical list for more than two weeks. It was interesting that even though our marriage was already splitting and we rarely prayed separately, much less together, there we stood outside Laurie's intensive care ward clinging to each other tightly and praying fervently with all our mights. The minute the crisis was over, however, we went back to fighting the cold war of emotional divorce.

Several years later after we had accepted Christ, we saw the emergence of a familiar pattern. Given a big crisis, we rushed, no, raced wildly into God's presence, sought His face, quoted Scripture, and almost immediately found His peace and lost our panic. However, if we had to face a daily trauma—a short, snide remark spoken by a Christian brother or sister or a bank teller asking for **more** identification before cashing our check—we went to pieces.

The key is in the words "we went." In one case we instantly went to the Lord; in the other, we went slowly and after much pessimistic brooding. What we lost by late action, besides valuable time, was the ability to cope. It never seems to occur to us in daily trivia to go immediately to the Lord with our attitudes and festering spirits.

For years I have been able to withstand the enormous pressures of traveling, but a number of years ago I regularly and habitually fell apart whenever the airlines lost my luggage.

Then once, when I landed in Atlanta—and my luggage went on to Puerto Rico—I was just about to dive into the pool of panic when, very quietly, I heard from within . . . "Why don't you run to Me and trust Me to do My work in you?"

I wondered what work the Lord could possibly do in me when my luggage, which was off vacationing in San Juan, held my clothes, my notes, and my well-marked Bible. But as it dawned on me that the Lord knew about this before it happened, I accepted the fact that He must have other plans. Calmly, I told the airline official where I would be speaking for the next three days and asked him to send my wayward suitcases over when they returned.

As it turned out, speaking in my slightly more than grubby pants suit and using no notes won the hearts of my non-Christian audience, and we saw God use the luggage loss, a most vexing daily problem, to His glory. To this day, each time an airline loses my luggage a small song starts inside of me. It's rather interesting to anticipate what new thing God is about to work.

I have to admit I wish I were this quick to run to Him on **all** daily vexations, but I **am** learning. The secret is to go immediately to the Lord. He wants us to be faithful in little things and to realize His sovereignty in all things. Evidently He wants to help us handle the dailies as well as the heavies, if we will turn to Him first.

We can grow through **differences** and through **daily** events and circumstances, and finally, believe it or not, we can grow through **doubt.**

Not long ago I watched a television documentary about Germany's Adolph Hitler. The film dealt with his early conquests. After he was shown as conqueror of the last country in a series of takeovers, the narrator said, "Now, with this latest triumph, Hitler took away the German people's freedom to doubt."

I was and still am fascinated with the phrase "freedom to doubt" because we usually do not associate freedom with doubt. It is safer by far to impose a "no freedom to doubt" rule; and Hitler, realizing this and not willing to risk the consequences, made sure that any doubt of his "right" to rule was not expressed openly. He removed the people's freedom to doubt.

Robert Browning once wrote,

> Who knows most,
> Doubts most.

In some circles it is a sin to doubt; yet often our times of doubt lead us on a search for truth, and once more the growing process is enhanced.

Several years ago one of our friends joined a religious cult. He jumped in with both feet and began an almost hysterical witnessing campaign to convert his friends. Dick and I knew we were on his list and sure enough one day, for four hours, he ranted and raved, produced seventeen Scriptures to every one of ours, and raised more doubts in our hearts than Carter has little liver pills.

"You are not believers," he shouted, pleaded, begged, and repeated. Dick's reaction was very German. He just got quiet and grew taller. My typical Irish-Hungarian temperament did its usual thing: flared, angered, simmered, and exploded in an endless cycle.

I will never forget our ride home after that ghastly afternoon. Our emotions ran from anger right straight to doubt. Our friend had used Scripture and had won every logical argument, and Dick and I were as defeated as any football team who has lost every game for three years straight. But a funny thing happened on our way to linking up with defeat.

When we got home we made a beeline for our Bibles to see exactly what we believed and why. Our doubt became the greatest motivation for spiritual growth that we had ever had.

Those terrible doubts forced us to search out the Word of God in a way neither of us ever could have guessed. For days, we read, prayed, and conversed about our faith, and when we emerged from the long tunnel of doubt, we knew once and for all where we stood as believers, why we believed as we did, what our theological positions were, and who we were when we called ourselves "children of God."

Our friend still tries to convert us from time to time, and he still thinks we are lost, but I love him because he made us doubt. He made us doubt the reality of Jesus as God, he cast doubts on our Christian daily life-style, and most assuredly he made the dubious prediction about our chances for eternal life. In short, he forced us to doubt our whole Christian experience, and God used that afternoon and several since to help us become even stronger in the Lord.

I am not blind to the destructive nature of doubt nor to how wrong it is to maintain a continually doubting spirit, but I do believe that God sometimes uses doubt to strengthen our faith.

I love the doubting disciple Thomas. I suspect that the reason he was allowed to see Jesus in person was precisely because he had so thoroughly doubted the other disciples' testimony regarding the Resurrection. I'm sure his faith was stronger and more durable after his personal encounter with the risen Christ.

I love, too, the attitude of the disciples toward Thomas' negative and doubting spirit. They didn't get angry with him; they didn't shut him off or ostracize him from their group of believing, excited hearts. They simply said, "Thomas, wait until you see Jesus for yourself." They knew Thomas' doubts would not be answered by human explanations, but by the Man Himself.

Sometimes God uses a person, an illness, an accident, the loss of a loved one, or the loss of a job to shake up the troops; but often the doubts such circumstances produce lead us to great harvests of growth.

These three "d's"—**differences, daily,** and **doubt**— can be stumbling blocks that trip us up every time we take a step. Or, they can be part of God's lovely path leading toward real growth. If we take that path we grow into the man or woman of God He wants us to be.

Chapter Seven

Growing Through Continuing

I would not give much for your religion
    unless it can be seen.
Lamps do not talk,
But they **do** shine.

> —Charles Haddon Spurgeon

Most of us, myself included, want to talk, write, or inform others of our faith. Very few of us want to be quiet, shining lamps, reflecting God's glory as Spurgeon has described.

Yet the growing process, as I have observed it for the past twenty years, is not always accomplished by great thrusts of movements, electrifying words or verbal exchanges, highly publicized preaching and gimmicks, or prolonged bursts of frenzied activity. More often than not—in fact, you could say it's the rule rather than the exception—Christian growing takes place during the

>   still quiet times of waiting
>   and our years of
>   simply continuing to continue.

My mother often remarked about the great many times God would seem to give the frustrating answer of "wait" to our prayers instead of a clearly defined, decisive yes or no. She was fascinated by the blocks of time a child of God spends in God's waiting room. In one place in her diary she wrote,

Christians today, as always, are waiting on God to answer their prayers. Many have waited long and have doubted God has heard. Others have become offended, especially when God has said "No," or worse yet, "Not now," and have charged God foolishly. When Job's whole life went out the window the Scripture says, "In all of this Job did not sin or charge God with wrong" (Job 1:22, RSV).

God's waiting room is the most tiresome and unpleasant place in our Christian experience. We do not like delays or denials, for hasn't God said, "Ask, and it shall be given you"? (Matt. 7:7). God has reasons for delays. Some He will reveal to us, others we may never know, but one thing we know for certain—God never makes a mistake!

Most of us know all about waiting rooms.

• If we are waiting in a doctor's office, we sit all glassy-eyed, idly thumbing through one magazine after another.

• If we are waiting in a restaurant for a table, we periodically hassle the hostess into showing us her list to prove she hasn't forgotten us.

• If we are waiting in our car trying to start it and the battery is dead, or the crossing light is stuck on red, our fingers drum out impatient tunes on our steering wheels. And the verbal language we use is not exactly lyrics for a musical.

• If we are left waiting in some hospital room or corridor for tests, X rays, or surgery, our spirits angrily question not only the whys, the financial cost of it all, but for the life of us we can't figure out this most inopportune delay.

• If you have ever waited on the Lord for a decision involving

deciding on a mate,
finding a job,
changing a career or vocation,
buying a house or car,
getting pregnant,
adopting a child,
recovering from major surgery or a coronary,

coping with a prodigal son or daughter,
working for disagreeable or unqualified people, or
adjusting to unfair or unjust situations,

then you can count yourself a member of a very large group.

In short, we are activists. We are not given to large amounts of tolerability when it comes to waiting or continuing. In our veritable storm of noisy activities and frantic desires to achieve success, we come to loathe the waiting-room experiences of life.

We stand up in church, discard our hymnal, and sing steadily and from memory,

> Have thine own way, Lord!
> Have thine own way.
> Thou art the potter,
> I am the clay.
>
> Mould me and make me after thy will,
> While I am waiting,
> Yielded and still.*

But as soon as church is over, we rush back out into our tense, stress-filled world, and we neither wait nor become yielded or still.

Our song, sung so valiantly in church, turns out to be nothing more than a flag of hypocrisy—gross, unattractive, and merely a flapping banner in the wind.

Why do we hate the waiting and the continuing experience so much? Why do we long to do anything but wait? What is it in our nature that drives us to productivity, speed, and impatience like a tennis ball volleying back and forth across the nets of life? Why is waiting or continuing so difficult a task? And why do we think that to be quiet or still at times shows some kind of lack of intelligence?

*G. C. Stebbins, "Have Thine Own Way, Lord" (Carol Stream, Ill.: Hope Publishing Co., 1935). (Original copyright 1907; renewed in 1935 by G. C. Stebbins.) Used by special permission.

I do not have the answers to these questions. However, I have had a lot of practice at waiting, and I can tell you this: I don't like waiting any more than you do. But I have learned and am satisfied knowing that the Lord uses our waiting-room experiences to bring about a new dimension in our growing.

Here are some observations about waiting and continuing that may help during your times of coping.

1. **Waiting out a time in God's waiting room never comes easily or automatically to any of us.**

Our attitude toward it will determine our demise or our development.

2. **The waiting process is used by God to force, slam, or shove us into a position of trust and dependence on Him.**

It is vital to our Christian experience to continually set our hearts on God in obedient trust and dependence. I wish we could all magically obey the Lord, do His will, and fall dutifully in line like good soldiers. But most of us, given that free will of ours, have to be forced into the waiting room before we give God our undivided attention! And sometimes we find we are not only to wait on the Lord, but also we're to take a back row seat, completely removed from the action!

Dick and I have become grandparents. Nine months ago our son and daughter-in-law presented us with a beautiful little granddaughter named April Joy.

No matter where I am or how busy my schedule is, I write April a letter each month. (Of course, April can't read, but her mother is saving the letters.)

About two months ago, little April had been visiting us on a Friday. Late that afternoon, her parents came to take her home. As she sat in her car seat, April helped me crystalize some thoughts on waiting, continuing, and taking a back seat.

On Sunday of that weekend, Dick and I left for San Francisco and I wrote April her monthly letter. I didn't intend to include my personal letter to her in a book, but because there is such confusion and anxiety about waiting, I thought it might help you clarify your think-ing on this subject.

Hi, darling girl,

The last I saw of you Friday, you were sitting all strapped and buckled in your car seat in the back of your parents' little red Volkswagen. You were not crying, fussing, or fidgeting, but you were definitely less than thrilled. You sat back there, your tiny mouth all set in a tight, grim little line, sober as a judge, and clearly you communicated,

1. I don't want to leave Grandma's house and go home.
2. I don't care for sitting back here while my parents ride up front and have all the fun!

You made my heart smile, darling girl, because I saw so much of me in you. I couldn't cajole you into a good-bye smile or wave at all, but I loved you so much in that moment because you pointed out a truth I needed to define a bit better.

You see, the noble truth is that much of life we sit in the back seat somewhere, buckled into our chairs alone and forced to wait it out. We are not sure what we are waiting for, but somehow we are forced into that undeni-able corner of trusting—because we have no other place to turn to!

So, trust you did! Not gleefully or with your usual joy-ous squealing, but respectfully, somberly, and with a will to continue. How dear you looked as you waited out your back-seat experience.

Believe it or not, your parents had your welfare clearly in mind, and even as you sat back there, not too sure of your parents' motives, they were taking excellent and loving care of you.

The seat straps and buckles were all for your protec-tion and safety. That car seat was not designed to im-prison or restrict you, but to **preserve** you.

Your parents drove you home because there they can best properly feed, bathe, and bed you down in your own sweet little white crib.

I see a perfect picture in this in regard to our relationship to God and His care of us. And I wonder why it is, when we think some cruel act of fate has us sitting all alone in the back seat or in some waiting room, that we are so hesistant to look forward? So reluctant to look in the seat ahead of us or to the side and see that God is definitely in the driver's seat and taking good care of us?

Darling girl, God was particularly watching over your precious family that very afternoon because while you sat back there waiting, unhappy, and full of unanswered questions, the Lord pointed out a small, charming house to a real estate lady and the next day the wheels were set in motion for your parents to have their very own first house. I know you don't know anything about California real estate but, baby, it's an outrageous, impossible problem. Yet God honored your parents' prayers and their waiting, and so your early life and future will be spent in that dear, treasured place.

There, you see? Even as you sat quietly questioning everything in the back seat, God was moving (literally) for your good.

He is a marvelous God, and the first prayer I will teach you to say is, "Jesus, I love you."

Grandpa and I are here in San Francisco for three days. Grandpa is working for the bank and I am (hopefully) writing another book—so I must get to it.

I love you, darling girl. Eat your vegetables as well as the yummies like peaches, pears and crunchy bread sticks!

Lovingly,
Grandma

Perhaps there is no way to come to a full position of trust except through the waiting-room and back-seat experiences.

As I look at the lives of marvelous, shining, lamp-like Christians of our times and biblical times, I see once more that growth, maturity, and spiritual accomplishments are achieved through waiting and continuing.

In a taped sermon called "Growing Through Waiting," my friend Pastor Chuck Swindoll made a survey of the Bible's wait-ers. His list included both the names of and the numbers of years each person mentioned spent buckled into the back seat somewhere:

Noah —who waited 120 years before it rained,

Job —who waited perhaps a lifetime, 60-70 years,

Abraham—who waited 100 years to find a city and never did,

Joseph —who served 14 years of imprisonment because of false accusations,

Moses —who waited 40 years in the desert.

I figured those years added up to over three hundred years of waiting, divided among five men. Then Pastor Swindoll mentioned in passing other wait-ers such as these Old Testament men: Samson, Samuel, Gideon, and the prophets. Rev. Swindoll also talked of New Testament men, starting with Jesus—who is the prime example of a wait-er—The Twelve, and Paul. Then he added this interesting zinger: "Most of the men who waited never realized their dreams or saw their hopes materialize."

How true. Perhaps this is exactly what we find the most difficult about waiting. We are deeply programmed to see the end product, the completion of a task, and the final outcome. In short, we are **result seekers, not continuers.** We have to be successful. We have to bring forth the evidence or we have failed in our mission. For the Christian that means producing so many born-again bodies, bringing so many new people to Sunday school, and adding names to the church membership roll. We seem to think that adding numbers is the only way to grow. But the man-made criteria for success and achievement are not God's ways.

Perhaps part of our confusion lies in the fact that there are many time lapses in the Bible. I'm not sure of the exact reason for it, but often the Word of God leaves out many years of ordinary, rather monotonous days of living.

Take, for example, Paul's missionary journeys. Those trips probably consumed the better part of thirty-five years of his life, yet the Scriptures appear to read as if it all happened within a three-year period. It's no wonder then when we read the account and see the achievements of Paul's "three-year" ministry, that we feel great frustrations because three years of our lives show so little in comparison. We become uptight with our lack of progress or our slow rate of growth because we want to live exciting, spiritual lives, and we feel we are not. We tend to forget that much of lives is made up of ordinary, uneventful days. As a woman, I think of waiting days as days filled not with writing books, having dinner with a publisher, speaking to a large audience or taping a television show, but with ironing, simmering stew on the back burner of my stove, and finally getting to the buttons and the mending.

We seem to show signs of irritability if our lives are narrowed down to a waiting-room period, a back-seat assignment, or a day intellectually limited by mundane chores. Yet, who among us could stand the strain of an exciting, miracle-a-minute existence?

Our Father who made us knew long before we arrived here that we would need the quiet, ordinary, even boring days to sit back, to put our confidence and trust in Him, and to learn about God's leading.

Evangelist Joe Arnett once said, "To learn God's will, take your gifts, buckle down, and use your talents in the local church as if you plan to stay there all your life. God will move you if He wants."

Over and over the psalmist talks of being still and waiting on the Lord. We must begin to see the times of waiting for what they really are: long-term growth.

Then too, there's the problem of our timing and God's timing. Unfortunately, God's timing never seems to line up with ours. We seem to beg Him for various things and we tell Him these are **needs,** not wants, and still **His** timing dictates the answers. I'm not sure why I have to relearn this concept about God's timing so many times a year, but I do.

Here is an interesting perspective put on our prayers and God's lesson in timing by my friend Ruth Calkin.

THANK YOU FOR WAITING

Had you given in to me, Lord
On the thing I wanted so much,
My life today
Would be a sorry mess.
I tell you nothing new—
I simply repeat
What you told me
Long, long ago.
Finally today I see it—
From your point of view.
Thank you for not giving in to me.
Thank you most of all
For patiently waiting
For me to give in to you.*

The line that touches me the most is "Thank you for not giving in to me." As I look back on my times of waiting and wanting, I see what a tragedy it would have been for God to have given in and released me from my waiting-room experiences.

Sometime, as a small project, write down some of the things you have begged God for and then count up how many times He didn't deliver your demands. As I read over my list, I could shout for joy because He denied my requests and kept me strapped in a back seat, out of action. Generally hindsight allows us to see the whole picture.

I am unashamedly and admittedly deeply in love with an Old Testament prophet named Habakkuk. He single-handedly has taught me more about using the

---

*Ruth Harms Calkin, Tell Me Again, Lord, I Forget (Elgin, Ill.: David C. Cook Publishing Co., 1974), p. 61. Used by permission.

waiting and continuing times and about trusting God with the "whole picture" concept than any man, dead or alive.

What a delightful, real honest-to-God man Habakkuk must have been. His book, fifth from the end of the Old Testament and only three chapters long, is a study in the frustrations of waiting and continuing without viable results.

Briefly, chapter 1 begins with Habakkuk shouting out about the "whys" of his life. Listen to his mounting frustration as he yells,

> O Lord, how long must I call for help before you will listen? I shout to you in vain; there is no answer. "Help! Murder!" I cry, but no one comes to save. Must I forever see this sin and sadness all around me?
>
> Wherever I look there is oppression and bribery and men who love to argue and to fight. The law is not enforced and there is no justice given in the courts, for the wicked far outnumber the righteous, and bribes and trickery prevail (Hab. 1:2–4, TLB).

Bless his dear heart. I know just how he felt. He had had it! He was sick of waiting around while all hell broke loose, while no one came to his rescue, and while evil enemies and their deeds prevailed.

The Lord's answer indicates that God was not angry or displeased with Habakkuk's outburst; but God's answer was of a most different vein than Habakkuk had expected. God proceeded to tell the prophet that things were going to get a **whole lot worse** before they got a whole lot better.

Habakkuk was genuinely shocked and I imagine his voice was choked with horror as he sputtered, "O, Lord my God, my Holy One, you who are eternal—is your plan in all of this to wipe us out? Surely not!" (Hab. 1:12, TLB).

And Habakkuk ends the first chapter with two burning questions to the Lord: "Will you let them get away with this forever? Will they succeed forever in their heartless wars?" (Hab. 1:17, TLB).

Clearly Habakkuk was as frustrated as you and I about life on this planet; yet somehow, someway he shook the cobwebs out of his mind and figured there were no options left, no courses of action open, and no alternatives available but **to wait on God.**

I can see him now, tugging on his full white beard and beginning the second chapter with his declaration, "I will climb my watchtower now, and **wait to see** what answer God will give to my complaint" (Hab. 2:1, TLB, emphasis mine).

Then gently Habakkuk records the voice of God saying,

"Write my answer on a billboard, large and clear, so that anyone can read it at a glance and rush to tell the others. But these things I plan won't happen right away. Slowly, steadily, surely, the time approaches when the vision will be fulfilled. If it seems slow, do not despair, for these things will surely come to pass. Just be patient! They will not be overdue a single day!

"Note this: Wicked men trust themselves alone [as the Chaldeans do], and fail; but the righteous man trusts in me, and lives!" (Hab. 2:2–4, TLB).

We have no way of knowing how long Habakkuk was silent before the Lord or how many days he waited there, for we have one of those time lapses again; but we do know God waited with him.

Habakkuk's lessons have taught me that:

• We have to wait in silence. Times of waiting are not the times to run here and there telling people our terrible tales of woe. These are not times to converge with close friends and engage in a pity party. Instead we are to be **still** and **know** that God is God, sovereign and sufficient for our ability to continue.

• We have to learn to blindly trust God **before we** see results or successful conclusions.

• We have to understand that no matter how dark the picture becomes, God will still be in control and will still be the **only** light of the world.

I am glad that darling Habakkuk did not end his book saying that everything had been worked out, that his enemies had been defeated, or that he was full of the right answers. On the contrary, while Habakkuk's last chapter is a song to be sung with soloists, choirs, and stringed instruments, he ends his book with these lyrics, "I will quietly wait for the day of trouble to come upon the people who invade us" (Hab. 3:16, TLB).

He writes his song not seeing results, not having achievements to present, and not experiencing a visible success. Yet he ends with,

> Even though the fig trees are all destroyed, and there is neither blossom left nor fruit, and though the olive crops all fail, and the fields lie barren; even if the flocks die in the fields and the cattle barns are empty, yet I will rejoice in the Lord; I will be happy in the God of my salvation. The Lord God is my Strength, and he will give me the speed of a deer and bring me safely over the mountains (Hab. 3:17–19, TLB).

He has decided to continue to continue. What a lesson! What a prophet! What a God! And the best news of all is that Habakkuk's God is still the same today.

For more than ten years now I have traveled extensively for the chaplains' division of the United States Army. I have spoken for large and small audiences of soldiers and their families, for military personnel in remote (even classified) bases, for the wives of military men in almost every state of the union, and I have taken four exhausting trips overseas. However, the military work—speaking and singing—that demanded the most from me in terms of energy, effectiveness, and real healing came from the speaking tours to the wards in military hospitals.

I have seen more waiting and continuing done in those hospitals than any place on the face of the earth.

In 1970, before the Vietnam conflict was drawn to a conclusion, I spoke in Japan at Camp Zama. I did many engagements there for military personnel, including women's luncheons, couples' banquets, high school assemblies, and seven wards of Camp Zama's hospital.

I set up a ward program with the chaplains that allowed me to sing four or five numbers in each ward. Then I would give a brief ten-minute testimony, and finally I was able to spend a few minutes bedside with as many boys as there was time for.

On the elevator in Zama's hospital, as we neared the floor where I was to do my very first military hospital performance, the Red Cross worker who accompanied the chaplains and me said rather casually, "The patients you'll be singing and speaking for are all in our open-wound wards, but we feel they need you the most." I nodded, feeling I could handle it. Little did I know.

I had not heard the term "open-wound ward" before, and even though I suspected what it meant I was in no way prepared for it. When we pushed through the first doors I saw before me men and boys fresh off the battlefield. Some had been air-lifted in only hours before and were still covered with Vietnam mud. Their bloody wounds were all uncovered, and the air was thick with the angry hopelessness of waiting.

Never had I felt so unequal to a task. My first thoughts were a sheer mess of panic-stricken, mumbled phrases.

But escaping was impossible, and so I smiled and stumbled over to the piano. The nurses pushed the ambulatory patients close beside me—and somehow, by the loving work of God, I swallowed the knot in my throat, tried to ignore the boy with half of his face covered with a bloody mass of pus, and sang my well-rehearsed numbers.

They were a marvelous, attentive, appreciative audience, and like all great audiences they began to pull the very best of everything from me.

I can never remember a time of singing any better, speaking and relating more directly to hurting hearts, or having a faster sense of humor. It was as if all my previous speaking and singing performances were merely a warm-up rehearsal for this one. This was the real thing, and God didn't waste one single experience or song or conversation between the soldiers and me.

That first day I laughed and cried with those men and sang and spoke in seven open-wound wards before noon.

It was in the last ward that morning, just before we left the hospital, that I felt compelled to turn and talk to just one more boy. I asked if there was time, and the chaplain glanced at his watch and okayed five more minutes.

In the first bed I saw, as I turned back to the ward, a young black soldier lay somberly looking at me. As I took the two or three steps to his side, I noticed he had no visible wounds or scars, and the blankets were neatly up around his chest.

I kidded him about his taking up a bed in this ward, when obviously there was nothing wrong with him. We teased back and forth for a minute and then I said, "Hey, no kidding, how come you're here? You look so well and I see no wounds."

He had been smiling, but he lost it and said quite simply, "Well, ma'am, the surgeons are upstairs right now, and they are deciding on whether or not they will amputate my legs. I'm just lyin' here waiting for their decision."

His words took my breath away, and I felt as if someone had swung a baseball bat directly to my middle.

"Is that scary?" was all I could manage.

"Yes, ma'am, it is," he answered.

I've never been in danger of losing an arm or leg or anything—except the end of my little finger once while

I was slicing a Christmas ham—and so I was at a loss to relate to him. But I asked, "How do you feel about it?"

"I guess I'm mad and a little bitter, ma'am," he said. "I've got a baby son whom I've never seen before and I don't want to go home half a man. If they take my legs off, they are going to do it here," he said, pointing to his thighs. "I don't want my kid to see no half a man. I want to be a whole man or I don't want to go home."

His face lost its pleasantness, and the anger of his words and feelings wrote themselves into his expression.

I honestly did not know how to respond to him, and to my surprise I found myself asking, "May I pray about this?"

Instantly, he said, "Oh, yes," and closed his eyes.

I felt idiotic, for there I stood, not having the slightest glimmer of insight on how to pray. I thought, I'm no Billy Graham. What am I doing here?

And then, because the Lord is our ever-present help in trouble, I remembered a part of a sermon our pastor preached before I left California. He said a psychiatrist in San Francisco had declared that man's greatest problem was his brokenness and that his greatest need was to be made whole.

So I began to pray. I don't remember the exact words, but I do remember most of the content. In general, here's how it went:

Oh, Lord, all morning I have seen broken men waiting for some kind of miracle. I've seen men without faces, arms, legs or parts of chests, stomachs or backs, and it has been horrible.

But worse than that, and sadder still, are the men who wait here with fragmented hearts, and shattered souls; hearts that have never known the forgiveness of God or never held the healing peace of God, and who never have experienced the wholeness of their manhood.

So, Lord, I don't know how to pray for the doctors upstairs, but I do know that You are the only one who can really make this man whole. You are the only forgiver of sins, the healer of wounds and giver of life; so touch this man, with or without his legs, and make him whole.

The soldier startled me by shouting not "Amen," but whooping out, "WOW! That's what I needed!"

Then he lifted up his head from the pillow and called loudly for the chaplains. It seemed to me that fifteen chaplains responded immediately, for we were instantly surrounded.

"Tell them upstairs, go up and tell them," he said excitedly, "that I can take their decision now. Whatever they decide, I can take it. I've been worrying about the wrong thing! I'm whole in here," he thumped his chest, "and that's what counts. So you go tell 'em—I'm ready."

It was the seventh time that morning my mascara and makeup were ruined. I stumbled out those doors, weeping and stunned with the way God operates.

One year later I returned to Japan and Camp Zama. When I got to the hospital I said to the first chaplain I met, "Say, do you remember a black soldier who was . . ." and the chaplain's face lit up like a Christmas tree.

"I've been waiting to tell you about him, Mrs. Landorf."

Then the chaplain told me that the doctors' verdict that day was not to amputate but to do surgery in a last ditch effort to save the soldier's legs. The surgery was a complete success, and six weeks later the soldier was sent home.

"But let me tell you about his last six weeks of convalescing here, Mrs. Landorf," the chaplain continued. "It was incredible! Even though he was in a wheelchair, he went to every ward in the hospital and told anyone who would listen, and a few who wouldn't, about the day he became 'whole.' He wrote his wife and family telling them of his conversion. He was almost hysterical with joy when he read a letter to me about his wife's

118

attendance at a little church and her acceptance of Christ. Mrs. Landorf, that soldier was the greatest thing that ever happened to this hospital, and none of us will ever forget him."

I have thought of that black soldier so many times. How he struggled with the waiting time, and yet God used both the wounds and the recovery period to make a whole man. What mysterious ways God devises and arranges for all of us, but how beautiful.

Did you know that God can give you a contentment in your waiting-room experience? Even though, like Habakkuk of old or the soldier of this century, you might not see the final result or hear the thunderous applause of success.

Are you fully aware that you have been born into God's family? You are planted in His garden, and it's exactly where He wants you, and for such a time as this!

Whether it's a waiting room or a harvest field, you may be in the only place that makes you totally accessible to God. Don't be discouraged, dear heart. It's God's place, too.

Paul said to his beloved friends at Philippi,

> And I am sure that God who began the good work within you will keep right on helping you grow in his grace until his task within you is finally finished on that day when Jesus Christ returns (Phil. 1:6, TLB).

There it is, the promise to help us grow, to help us endure, to help us not self-destruct in times of stress; and the promise is good for as long as it takes for Christ to return.

David said it beautifully when he said,

> But the godly shall flourish like palm trees, and grow tall as the cedars of Lebanon. For they are transplanted into the Lord's own garden, and are under his personal care. Even in old age they will still produce fruit and be

THE HIGH COST OF GROWING

vital and green. This honors the Lord and exhibits his
faithful care. He is my shelter. There is nothing but goodness in him! (Ps. 92:12–15, TLB).

Oh, Lord, thank you for all these different ways of
growing. Help us to learn our lessons well, for when
we are obedient to you our joy knows no boundaries,
our love sets no limits, and wisdom ever broadens.
But we need you, Lord.
Help us to continue to continue to continue. . . .

S0-AKN-010

Auto Repair for Dummies

Glove Compartment Guide

Auto Repair for Dummies
Glove Compartment Guide

Deanna Sclar

Ten Speed Press
Berkeley, California

TEN SPEED PRESS
P.O. Box 7123
Berkeley, CA 94707

Library of Congress Cataloging-in-Publication Data

    The glove compartment guide for dummies / by Deanna Sclar.

       p.   cm.
    ISBN 0-89815-435-9
    1. Automobiles—Maintenance and repair—Amateurs' manuals. I. Title.
    TL152.S423 1991
    629.28'722—dc20   91-13576
                                        CIP

Book design and typography by Canterbury Press
Cover Design by Fifth Street

Printed in the United States of America

    3 4 5 – 95 94 93

For Jesse Ché

May you walk in beauty

Contents

Introduction

Since the first edition of *Auto Repair for Dummies* hit the stands back in 1976, over half a million readers have lugged the book around in their cars like a security blanket. Since *Dummies* runs to almost 500 pages, that's quite a bit of excess baggage, so here's a much more portable and vastly abridged version, designed to help you prevent breakdowns and deal with them if they occur anyway.

Of course, the best way to prevent trouble is regular maintenance, and the big edition of *Auto Repair for Dummies* has easy, detailed instructions for doing that yourself, more cheaply and quickly than taking the car to a mechanic. You'll find notes on where to find pertinent instructions for maintenance and repair in *Dummies* throughout this little guide and, for those who like a little comedy with their information, there's an "Auto Repair for Dummies" home video.

Even the best maintained cars can meet with the unexpected, and this little book should prove to be your best friend on the road. Read it through once, follow its preventive procedures, then tuck it away in the glove compartment and relax knowing you can handle the unforeseen without losing your cool.

Best regards,

Deanna Sclar

PART I

Before You Start Out

The best way to deal with problems on the road is to avoid them in the first place. Consequently, before you start out, there are a couple of things you can do to either prevent problems from happening, or make handling them a lot easier.

Pack a Bag for Your Car

It's bad enough to have something go wrong with your car while you're on the road, but if you have to wait hours for a tow truck, or can't get at what you need just to correct a simple problem, you really are going to be miserable. So keep the following items in your car where you can get at them easily:

Jacks

Keep a jack in your vehicle at all times. It's depressing to try to fix a flat only to find you've left the jack at home.

Scissor Jack   Hydraulic Jack
Types of Jacks

3

Check your jack periodically and lubricate it. If you need to buy one, be sure it's suited to your car's bumper design. I like the little hydraulic ones; they're not very expensive.

Fire Extinguishers

A fire extinguisher is a *must* for your car. Get the 2¾-pound dry chemical type. Engine fires do not necessarily mean that the car is ruined—if you can put them out quickly. Cigarette butts can land on your back seat, and fires can be caused by ruptured fuel lines, flooded carburetors, and faulty wiring, so an inexpensive fire extinguisher may not only save you money; it may also save your life. If the flames are anywhere near the fuel tank, however, forget the heroics; just run for it and throw yourself to the ground if you think it might explode. Because your fuel tank is located right under your trunk compartment, keep your extinguisher under the front seat of your car, in a suitable bracket. Otherwise, it can roll under the pedals in normal stopping.

Funnels

Funnels are used for filling your radiator, adding oil, and adding transmission fluid to your car. Either metal or plastic is fine.

Flares and Flashlights

A flashlight is always a good addition to your glove compartment. It will help your kids to locate dropped toys on the floor of the car, enable you to see under the hood if your car breaks down, and serve as an emergency light for oncoming traffic if you have to stop on the highway for repairs. Flares can be dangerous, and many states have rules regarding their use on the highways. A flashlight with a red blinker is safer, more versatile, and just as good. Carry a couple of fresh batteries.

Rags

Rags should be clean and lint-free. Keep a clean rag in your glove compartment; you'll need it (if for nothing else) to defog your windshield.

Spare Tires

Check your spare tire often. It is humiliating to go through the work of changing a tire only to find that your spare is flat, too. If your spare is worn beyond belief, most garages will sell you a not-too-hideous patched tire at a low price.

Lug Wrenches

A lug wrench is sometimes provided, along with the jack, on new cars. It is used to remove the wheel or lug nuts when you change your tires. But if you are going out to buy a lug wrench, get the *cross-shaft* kind. It will provide you with more leverage.

Cross-Shaft Lug Wrench

Jumper Cables

One of the most common malfunctions of a car is the loss of power to start it, either from an old or faulty battery or because you've left the headlights on by mistake. Once in this situation, you can either wait for the AAA or a nearby garage to come and bail you out, or you can stop a passing car, whip out your jumper cables, attach them in seconds, and "jump a start" from the Good Samaritan's car to your own. Full instructions for the proper way to "jump a start" can be found on page 72.

First-Aid Kit

Nothing fancy. A couple of Band-Aids, something soothing for burns, and a good antiseptic will do.

Hand Cleaner

A small tube for quick clean-ups. Some brands remove grease from your clothes and tar from your feet, too.

Gloves

Thin, tough, and comfortable surgical gloves are available at any pharmacy. They cost little and will keep the grease out from under your fingernails.

Spare Tools

A couple of screwdrivers (or one that comes with interchangeable heads), an adjustable wrench, a spark-plug socket, and a can of penetrating oil come in handy.

Other Useful Goodies

▷ A couple of old spark plugs that have been gapped properly
▷ An old set of points
▷ A spare fan belt (tow trucks don't carry them)
▷ A tire gauge
▷ Extra fuses
▷ A can of inflater/sealant for flats that occur when you can't change a tire on the spot
▷ Tinfoil to prevent vapor lock on extra hot days

▷ Your owner's manual
▷ The service manual for your car

If You're Heading Off the Beaten Path

As the enlightened gurus of the East say, "On any path the Way is of more importance than the Goal." This is especially true of long-distance car trips. If getting there and back again is dismal, the short time you spend enjoying the object of your journey often is simply not worth the effort. The key to happy tripping lies less in *how much* you take than in *what* you take and *how* you pack it. It is important to travel light for fuel economy, since it takes gasoline to lug every pound around. How then do you evaluate what you need and what you can leave behind? Here are a couple of tips that work for me:

Your car may be the most important member of your entourage. See that it is roadworthy and be sure to pack its necessities as well as those of the others making the trip. Check the car out thoroughly to be sure it's ready for the road. Do this a couple of days beforehand to provide time to handle any problems you discover. Use the following as a checklist:

Tires

1. Check the treads for signs of misalignment, following the instructions in this chapter. A couple of hundred miles

at highway speeds can finish off a pair of new radials if they are out of alignment.

2. Check also to be sure that the tires have enough tread left to make the trip. It's better to buy a new set early when you can shop for the best prices than to risk the dangers of a blowout in some out-of-the-way place where tires (and medical help) may not be readily available!

3. Check the sidewalls of your tires to see if you can add a few extra pounds of air pressure to help you carry an extra-heavy load. Don't exceed the maximum embossed on the tire. If you are going to be driving where it is very hot, remember that hot air expands and the pressure inside the tires will rise along with the thermometer. The same goes for high-speed driving—freeway speeds dramatically increase the heat and pressure in your tires. Check them in the morning when they're cold to be sure that they are not too far over or under the limits. This will extend the life of the tires and give you the best ride and maximum fuel efficiency. Generally speaking, nothing horrible will happen if your tire pressure goes a bit over the maximum when it gets hot, as long as both tires on an axle remain equal in pressure. If you find excessively unequal pressure developing in a tire, have it checked for a slow leak or for damage to the inside of the tire. DON'T FORGET TO CHECK YOUR SPARE TIRE!

Cooling System

If you haven't changed the coolant and flushed the cooling system in a year, do it now, especially if you are going to be traveling to an area with extremely high or low temperatures. Easy instructions start on page 175 of *Auto Repair for Dummies*.

Under-the-Hood Check

Go through the complete under-the-hood check in this chapter. It will prevent about 70 percent of the problems that cause highway breakdowns. This may be the most important thing you do to prepare for any trip!

Give the Car a Tune-up

This is no time to get lazy. Take the time to tune the car before you leave. Proper carburetor adjustments, clean spark plugs, and accurate timing will really pay off in fuel economy and performance, and that couple of extra miles to the gallon really adds up to big savings on long trips!

Stash Some Extras for Emergencies

If you're planning a long trip, or heading away from civilization, add the following:

▷ An old rotor and condensor
▷ Spare radiator hoses
▷ A can of engine oil

▷ A can of brake fluid
▷ Roadside reflectors (they're safer than flares)
▷ A gallon of water
▷ A small, lightweight, collapsible shovel
▷ Tire chains, a small bag of sand, and an extra blanket if you're headed for snowy areas

Under-the-Hood Check

We all know chronic "tire kickers" who habitually walk around their car, kicking the tires to make sure they aren't flat, before they get in and drive off. We tend to laugh at them, and yet they probably are rarely caught with flat tires. We can learn a little from these people and make a habit of checking the little things under the hood of our cars—maybe not *every* time we go anywhere, but definitely once a month and before starting out on long trips. I've provided a Maintenance Record at the back of *Auto Repair for Dummies* to help you keep track of what you've checked and what you've replaced. You might want to keep a copy of it in your car.

Safety Rules

Before we go any further, I'd like to give you a few safety rules for working on your car:

1. Tie back long hair. If it accidentally gets into a moving fan or belt you can literally be scalped.

2. Never work on your car unless the parking brake is on, the car is in either "Park" or "Neutral," and the engine is shut off. If you have to run the engine to adjust something, turn it on and off yourself to avoid the risk that a friendly helper may misunderstand and turn the engine on while your hands are in the way.

3. Never jack a car up unless the wheels are properly blocked. I'll go into this when we talk about changing tires.

4. Use insulated tools for electrical work.

5. Before using a wrench or ratchet on a part that is "stuck," be sure that, if it suddenly comes loose, your hand won't hit anything. To avoid this, *pull* on wrenches whenever possible, rather than *push* them.

6. Be sure the parts of the engine you are working on are nice and cold, so you won't get burned. If you are doing a job that calls for a warm engine, be very careful.

7. Don't smoke when you are working on your car—for obvious reasons!

So much for the scary stuff. It's all a matter of common sense, really. And remember, it is almost impossible to make a car "blow up" unless you drop a match into the gas tank. If you do something incorrectly, the worst thing that will probably happen is that the car won't start until you get it right. The first time I tuned my car I was sure that if I made the smallest mistake the car would explode when I started it. This seems to be a common delusion. It just isn't so. All you'll get is silence (which can be just as disconcerting, but not lethal, after all). And now, to work.

How to Open the Hood of Your Car

Obviously, in order to check under the hood you have to know how to get it open. Oddly enough, many people haven't the faintest idea how to do that, and it differs from car to car. You can consult your owner's manual, if you have one, or ask the service station attendant to show you how the next time you go in for gas, but if you're really feeling adventurous, try this:

1. Look around and through the grill to find a handle, lever, arm, or button, or feel under the grill and behind the bumper for a handle or lever. Then, pull, press, push front to back and side to side on the thing you find. The hood should open a little, but it may be stopped by a safety catch that prevents it from coming open, and obscuring your vision, while you are driving.

2. Raise the hood with one hand, and feel along the underside for a metal lever which, when pressed one way or the other, releases the catch. Then raise the hood the rest of the way.

3. If it stays up, fine. If not, look for a safety rod attached

to the underside of the hood. This should come down and fit into a slot. Other rods lift up from the frame and fit into a slot under the hood.

Now that you know how to get under the hood, here's what you should check:

Radiator Check

1. If your car has a coolant recovery reservoir (a plastic bottle connected to the radiator that holds an extra supply of liquid), there is no need to open the radiator cap. Just check to see if the liquid reaches the level indicated on the bottle, and remove the bottle cap to check the quality of the liquid inside. If there is no coolant recovery bottle, open the cap on your radiator and check to see if the water in it is running low. You should be able to see the water a couple of inches below the cap. If the level is low, add water or coolant. Tap water is fine. You should always do this when the engine is cold, to avoid the possibility of being burned. If you ever have to remove a radiator cap from a car that has been running, be sure to see page 94 for instructions.

2. If the liquid looks pink, green, or yellow that's the coolant, or antifreeze. If it looks rusty or has things floating around in it, you should flush your radiator and add new coolant. Instructions for when and how to do this can be found on page 175 of *Auto Repair for Dummies*.

3. While you are messing around with your radiator,

feel the big hoses that go into the top and come out of the bottom of the radiator. If they are leaking, cracked, bulgy, or squishy, they should be replaced. Easy instructions begin on page 171 of *Dummies*.

How to Check and Tighten a Fan Belt

Take a look at the belt that goes around the fan and the alternator (or generator) on your car. Is it cracked or frayed inside or outside? If it is, it should be replaced. Is the inside of the belt glazed and shiny? This means it should be replaced, too. Does the belt "give" more than half an inch when you press on it midway between the alternator and the fan? You might be able to adjust it if the belt is otherwise in good condition.

Here's how to tighten your fan belt:

1. Loosen the nuts and bolts that secure the alternator bracket.

2. Pull the alternator back, away from the fan end of the belt, so that the belt is drawn tighter. Then tighten the nuts and bolts. Check again after about 100 miles of driving to see if it has loosened again.

Keep the old belt in the trunk of your car for emergencies. If replacing it yourself does not seem worth the effort, you can have the fan belt adjusted or replaced at almost any service station.

Battery Check

1. Open those little caps, or remove the bars, on the top of your battery. Look inside. If you can see the tops of the plates inside the battery, add distilled water or water with a low mineral content. (If you have a sealed battery, you will not be able to do this.)

Caution: Never open a battery with a lighted cigarette in your mouth. For that matter, don't smoke when working around your car. Batteries are filled with acid, which generates hydrogen gas, so you want to be careful when working around them.

2. The cruddy deposits that form in lovely colors on the top of your terminals are made by this acid. Brush it off with a wire *battery brush*, or remove it with some baking soda and water. Try to avoid getting the powdery stuff on your hands or clothes, but if you do, just wash it off with water *right away* and neither you nor your clothes will be damaged. If you coat the terminals with grease or petroleum jelly, you can help to prevent these deposits from forming.

3. Check to see that the wires leading to the terminals are not frayed. If they are, they should be replaced, or the battery may short circuit. By the way, if those caps or bars look beyond help, you can buy replacements cheaply at the auto supply store.

4. If your battery has been acting up lately—if you are having trouble starting your car or your lights dim out—or if the battery is very old, buy a battery tester

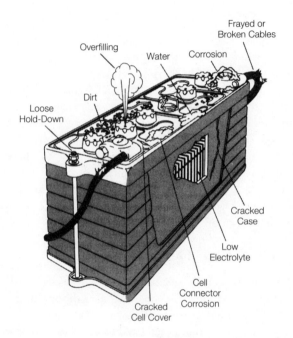

and check to see if the acid level is high enough. These testers cost only a few dollars, and you simply draw some of the battery fluid into the tester and look at the floating balls inside it. A scale on the tester will tell you the condition of the battery fluid. If you get a very low reading, you can get the fluid changed at a service station. But if they tell you that the condition of the plates inside the battery is also deteriorating, you are probably going to have to buy a new one.

Hose Check

Walk around the hood area, squeezing every hose you encounter. If you meet any that are leaking, bulgy, soft and squishy, or hard and brittle, turn to Chapter 8 of *Dummies* for instructions on how to replace them. Replacing a hose is an easy job. It pays to replace hoses *before* they break; any saving of time or effort is not worth the aggravation of having your trip come to an abrupt stop on the freeway because of a broken hose. Most emergency trucks do not carry spare hoses, and you may end up paying an expensive tow charge for a couple of dollars' worth of hose that could have been replaced in about 10 minutes, if you'd kept a spare in the trunk.

How to Check and Add Oil

Sticking out of the side of the engine block is a little dipstick with a ring on the end of it. That's the one the gas station attendant is always showing you and saying, "Looks like it needs oil. Shall I add some?" Now, look at it yourself. First, be sure that your engine is cold or has been shut off for a few minutes. Then, pull the little stick out and wipe it off on a clean rag. Now shove the stick back in again. If it gets stuck on the way in, turn it around. The pipe it fits into is curved, and the metal stick will bend naturally in the direction of the curve if you put it back the way it came out. Now pull it out again and look at the tip of the stick. You will see a film of oil. Does the oil film reach only to where it says "add oil" on the dipstick?

Or does it reach to where it says "full"? Is the film of oil on the dipstick very black and gooky? Stick the tip of your finger in it. Does it leave your fingertip dirty when you wipe it off? Then you should probably have your oil changed. Chapter 12 of *Dummies* will tell you how to change your oil yourself. It's easy and will save you a lot of money.

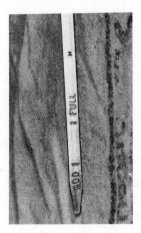

An Oil Dipstick

Let's say that your oil looks clean enough but that it only reaches to the "add oil" level on the dipstick. You can get some oil next time you fill up at the gas station, or you can buy a can at the auto supply store and add it yourself. Check your owner's manual for the proper weight of oil for your car. 10-40 is usually OK.

Here's how to add oil:

1. Remove the cap from the oil filler hole at the top of your engine. This large cap is easy to recognize: it lifts or screws right off, revealing a largish hole.

2. Use a funnel, or just good aim, to pour fresh oil into the oil filler hole.

3. Add a little at a time and keep checking the dipstick until the oil reaches the "full" line. Be sure not to overfill; you can damage your engine if you do.

4. Don't forget to replace the oil filler cap, or you'll find oil splashed all over the engine compartment the next time you open the hood!

How to Check and Replace Your Air Filter

If you unscrew the wing nut on the lid of your air cleaner and undo any other devices that hold it down, you will find an air filter inside. Although most cars come with dough-nut-shaped, pleated-paper filters that can be replaced for a few dollars, a few older models have permanent air filters, which should be cleaned according to instructions in your owner's manual.

To see whether your air filter needs replacement, just lift it out (it isn't fastened down) and hold it up to the light. Can you see the light streaming through it? If not, try dropping it *lightly*, bottom side down, on the ground. This should jar some dirt loose. Don't blow through it—you can foul it up that way. If it is still too dirty to see through after you've dropped it a few times, you need a new one.

It's a good idea to change these filters at least every year or every 20,000 miles, whichever comes first—unless yours gets very dirty before then. If you do most of your driving in a dusty or sandy area, you may need to replace your air filter every 5,000 miles, or less.

To replace your air filter, just go to your local auto supply store, tell them the make, model, and year of your car, buy a new one, take the old one out, and drop the new one in. Look for well-known, quality-brand filters; you can often get them quite cheaply at a discount store.

The Air Filter is Inside the Air Cleaner

Unknown brands sell for very little, but they are not always of good quality, and if your air filter lets a lot of junk get into your carburetor, you may find that a cheap filter is very costly in the long run. Be sure the filter you get matches your old filter in size and shape. That way you'll be sure you've been sold the proper filter for your car.

Brake Fluid Inspection

On the driver's side of your car, usually up near the firewall, is a little box or bottle with pipes, or a pipe, coming from it. This is your master cylinder. It holds the brake fluid that gets pushed down the lines to each wheel of your car when you step on the brake pedal. If there is insufficient brake fluid, your car won't stop properly. Here's how to check the level of brake fluid in your master cylinder:

1. Open the top of your master cylinder. If you have the kind with a little plastic bottle on top, just unscrew the cap. If you have a metal one, use a screwdriver to pry the retaining clamp off the top. Be sure not to let any dirt fall into the chambers when you open the lid. If your hood area is full of funky grime and dust, wipe the lid before you remove it.

2. Take a look at the lid. Attached to the inside surface is a rubber diaphragm with two rubber cups. As the brake fluid in your master cylinder recedes (when it is forced into

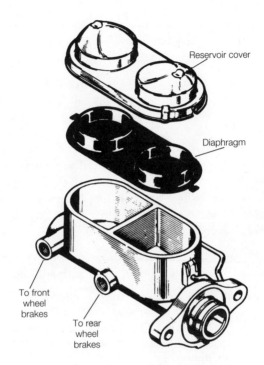

Dual-Chamber Master Cylinder

the brake lines), the diaphragm cups are pushed down by air that comes in through vents in the lid. The rubber cups descend and touch the surface of the remaining brake fluid, to prevent evaporation and to keep the dust and dirt out. When the fluid flows back in, the rubber cups are pushed back up. If your fluid level is low, or if the rubber cups are in their descended position when you remove the lid, you will have to push them back up with your finger before you replace the lid.

3. Look inside the master cylinder. The brake fluid should be up to the fill line or within half an inch of the top of the chamber. If it isn't, you will have to buy brake fluid and add it.

A low brake-fluid level may not mean anything if it has been a long time since any fluid was added, and if your car has been braking properly. If you have reason to believe that your brake fluid level has dropped because of a leak, then check the rest of your system very carefully. Chapter 10 of *Dummies* shows you how to do this.

If you need to add brake fluid, be sure you buy the proper kind. Here are some things you should know:

   a. Always use top-quality brake fluid from a well-known manufacturer. Brake fluid for disc brakes has a higher boiling point than brake fluid designed for drum brakes and can be used on cars with any kind of brakes. However, drum brake fluid cannot be used with disc brakes.

   b. If you have front disc brakes and rear drum brakes on your car, you probably have disc brake fluid in both chambers of your master cylinder.

   c. *This is important!* Brake fluid becomes swiftly contaminated by exposure to air.

The oxygen in the air oxidizes it and lowers its boiling point. It also has an affinity for moisture, and the water vapor in the air can combine with the brake fluid to form ice crystals that make braking difficult in cold weather. If you add water-vapor-contaminated fluid to your brake system, it can rust the system and create acids that will etch your wheel cylinders and master cylinder and foul your brakes, causing them to work poorly—or not at all. Therefore, if you are going to add brake fluid to your system, buy a small can, add the fluid to your master cylinder, and *throw the rest away*, or use it only in emergencies.

4. If both chambers of your master cylinder are filled with brake fluid to the proper level, close it up carefully, without letting any dirt fall into it. If dirt gets into your master cylinder, it will travel down the brake lines. If it doesn't block them, the dirt will end up in your wheel cylinders and damage your brakes.

5. Remember, brake fluid evaporates easily, so don't stand around admiring the inside of your master cylinder. Close it quickly, and be sure that the cover is securely in place. Since most master cylinders are pretty airtight, you should not lose brake fluid in any quantity unless it is leaking out somewhere else. If your fluid level was low, we'll find the cause as we continue to check the system.

6. Take a flashlight, or a work light, and look for stain marks, wetness, or gunk under the master cylinder and on the firewall near it. If your master cylinder is—or has been—leaking, there will be evidence.

7. It's a good idea to check your master cylinder every couple of months; more often if it was low in fluid when you last checked it. This should be part of your regular under-the-hood check.

Automatic Transmission Fluid Check

If your car has an automatic transmission, it's a good idea to do this regularly. People have paid to have their transmissions rebuilt when a quart of transmission fluid would have saved them the expense.

1. Look for the dipstick handle sticking out of your transmission. Since there are many different kinds of transmissions in use these days, check your owner's manual to locate your dipstick and to learn which type of fluid your car requires. If you have no manual, ask your local car dealer.

2. Let your engine run with the car in "Neutral" or "Park." Be sure your emergency brake is on. When the car is warm, leave the engine running and pull out the dipstick. Wipe it with a clean, lint-free rag. Reinsert it and pull it out again. If the stick shows that you need more transmission fluid, use a funnel to pour just enough fluid

down the dipstick tube to reach the "full" line on the stick. Do not overfill!

3. If the transmission fluid on the dipstick looks or smells burnt or has particles in it, have the fluid drained and changed by a mechanic. It should be pinkish and almost clear.

4. Be sure to shut off your engine before proceeding with the rest of this checkup.

Power-Steering Fluid Check

Locate the power-steering pump in your car. Your owner's manual should tell you where it is. Unscrew the cap and check to see that the fluid is up to the fill mark on the dipstick, or near the top of the bottle. If it isn't, check your owner's manual to see what kind of fluid it requires.

NOTE: If any of the water, oil, transmission, brake, or power-steering fluid levels are very low and it has been only a short time since that particular fluid was added to your car, it might be a wise idea to find out why you are losing fluid.

Windshield Washer Fluid Check

Under your hood there is a plastic bottle or bag that connects to the washers on your windshield wipers. Is it full of liquid? If not, you can fill it with any one of a variety of windshield washer solutions. Don't use detergent. It can leave a residue that can plug up your lines, and it isn't easy to drive with suds all over your windshield!

If your wipers have been making a mess of your windshield, buy new blades for them. These are generally inexpensive, and usually just slide or snap into place. Consult your owner's manual, if you can't figure it out by looking—or ask the person in the auto parts store to tell you how the blades are inserted.

Wiring Check

Feel the wires that you encounter under the hood. If they feel hard and inflexible, if there are bright metal wires showing through the insulation, or if the wires look corroded or very messy where they attach to various devices, they may need to be changed before they short out. Have a garage do the rewiring until you really get to be an expert.

How to Check Your Tires and Add Air

Buy an accurate tire gauge (they aren't expensive) and check the pressure in each of your tires.

1. To determine the proper air pressure for your tires, look for "MAX PRESS" on the sidewalls to see how many pounds per square inch (psi) they should contain.

Some tires give you a minimum amount, as well. Some manufacturers suggest you put more air in the front tires than in the rear ones, for easier handling and better traction. Keep the tires on the same axle at equal pressure.

2. Remember that in hot weather the pressure in your tires will rise as the air in them heats up and expands. This is also true after you have heated up your tires with a lot of driving, so check tire pressure in the morning before you use the car.

3. Remove the little cap from the tire valve that sticks out of your tire near the wheel rim. There is no need to remove your hub cap to do this.

4. Place the rounded end of the tire gauge against the valve so that the little pin in the gauge contacts the pin in the valve.

5. Press the gauge against the valve stem. You will hear a hissing sound as the air starts to escape from the tire.

6. At this point, you will see a little stick emerge from the other end of the tire gauge. It will emerge partway almost as soon as the air starts to hiss, and it will stop emerging almost immediately. Without pushing the stick back in, remove the gauge from the tire valve.

7. Look at the stick without touching it. There are little numbers on it, and the last number showing is the amount of air pressure in your tire. Is it the right amount? If it seems too low, press the gauge against the valve stem

again. If it still doesn't move, you need more air. Do this for each tire, and don't forget the spare!

8. If your tires appear to be "low," note the amount that they are underinflated, then drive to your local gas station. At this writing, it costs nothing to use the air hose at most stations. Isn't it nice to know that some things are still free? But, since it's free, you're probably going to want to do it yourself. Here's how:

a. Remove the cap from the tire valve.

b. Check the air pressure in the tire with *your* gauge to see how much it's changed so you can add the same amount of air the tire lacked before you drove to the station.

c. Add air in short bursts, checking each time with *your* tire gauge. The gauges on many station air hoses have been found to be inaccurate.

d. If you add too much air, let some out by depressing the pin on the tire valve with the back of the air hose nozzle or with the little knob on the tire gauge.

e. Check again until you've got it right. No one hits it on the head the first time.

Check Your Tires for Wear

If you want to determine whether or not you should (a) buy new tires, (b) have your wheels balanced, (c) have your front end aligned, or (d) change your driving habits, you can tell a lot by simply reading your tire treads for clues. The chart on this page and the illustration on the next page will show you what to look for.

How to Read Your Treads

Clue	Culprit	Remedy
Both edges worn	Underinflation	Add more air Check for leaks
Center treads worn	Overinflation	Let air out to manufacturer's specifications
One-sided wear	Poor alignment	Have wheels aligned
Treads worn unevenly, with bald spots, cups, or scallops	Poor alignment	Have wheels aligned
Edges of front tires only worn	You are taking curves too fast	Slow down!
Saw-toothed wear pattern	Poor braking habits	Learn to pump your brakes or slow down
Whining, thumping, and other weird noises	Poor alignment, worn tires or shocks	Have wheels aligned or buy new tires or shocks
Squealing on curves	Poor alignment or underinflation	Check wear on treads and act accordingly

1. Look at each tire. Are there nails, stones, or other debris embedded in the treads? Remove them. *But*, if you are going to remove a nail, first be sure your spare tire is inflated and in usable shape. If, when you pull a nail, you

hear a hissing sound, push the nail back in quickly and take the tire to be fixed. If you aren't sure if air is escaping, put some water on the hole and look for the bubbles made by escaping air. If you're still not sure whether the thing may have caused a leak, check your air pressure and then check it again the next day to see if it is lower. Tires with leaks should be patched by a professional. If the leak persists, get a new tire.

It's Time for New Tires When
Tread-Wear Indicators Appear

2. Look at the treads again. Most tires have tread-wear indicators built into them. These are bars of hard rubber that appear across treads that have been worn down to $\frac{1}{16}$ of an inch of the surface of the tire. If these indicators appear in two or three different places, less than 12 degrees apart on the circumference of the tire, the tire should be replaced. If your tires don't show these indicators and you think they are worn, place a thin ruler into the tread and measure the distance from the base of the tread to the surface. It should be more than $\frac{1}{16}$ of an inch deep.

3. If your front tires are more worn than your rear ones and show an abnormal wear pattern, you probably need to have your wheels aligned.

4. If you keep losing air in your tires, have your local service station check them for leaks. Sometimes a leak is caused by an ill-fitting rim. The garage has a machine that can fix this easily.

5. If the garage cannot find a leak and if your rims fit properly, and you are still losing air, you probably have a faulty tire valve that is allowing air to escape. You can buy snap-in tire valves to replace the ones on your car. Look for the number molded into the base of the tire valves on your car; then buy new ones. At least one of the four valve caps should have a notched end for removing and replacing tire valves. If you don't have one, buy one.

Check the Lug Nuts

Mechanics usually use power tools to tighten the lug nuts that hold your car's wheels in place. It's miserable to have to change a flat on the road and find that you can't get the @#$% nuts loose. To prevent this problem, try to loosen the nuts now, following the directions in Part III. If they are on so tight that you can't break them loose, find a piece of pipe, fit it over the shaft of your lug wrench, and use it for a lever. After you loosen each nut, tighten it yourself, following the instructions in Part III. Now you'll be able to get them off easily if you have to change a flat on the road.

Overnight Check for Leaks

Park your car over a clean patch of driveway, leave it overnight, and check to see if there is any liquid on the ground under it in the morning.

1. If it's black and greasy, and under the engine area, it's oil. Open the hood and check around and under the engine to find the source.

2. If it's pinkish and greasy, check to see which part of the car it's under, to find out whether it's transmission or power steering fluid.

3. If it's a pool of greenish or yellowish liquid and it's under the engine compartment, it's coolant. Check the

hoses, the radiator, and the water pump to find the source of the leak.

4. Liquid near a tire can be one of two things:

a. If it's down the inside of the tire, it's probably brake fluid from a leaky wheel cylinder.

b. If it's down the outside of the tire it's probably a dog...

"Auto Repair for Dummies: The Maintenance Tape" has a more detailed sequence about this type of checkup and Chapter 8 of *Auto Repair for Dummies* has a wealth of information on tracing and fixing leaks.

Buying Parts for Your Car

If these checks have revealed the need to replace parts or fluids, you'll need to know certain information in order to buy the ones specifically designed for your car. That information is called "specifications," and every auto parts store has a "spec sheet" that shows parts numbers of various vehicles based on these specifications:

1. The *manufacturer's name* (General Motors, etc.)

2. The *make* of the car (Pontiac, etc.)

3. The *model* of the car (Firebird, etc.)

4. The *year* the car was built

5. The number of *cylinders* in the car (4, V8, etc.)

The following are not always necessary, but may be essential for buying certain parts:

6. The *horsepower* rating

7. If the car has a *carburetor* (as opposed to fuel injection) how many barrels does it have?

8. Does it have an automatic or manual *transmission*?

9. Is it *air-conditioned*?

Where to Find Specifications

All this information should be in your owner's manual, and most of it is also printed on metal tags or patches located inside your hood. These can be found in front of the radiator, inside the fenders, on the inside of the hood, anywhere the auto manufacturer thought you'd find them. I know of one car that has its patch inside the lid of the glove compartment. Look around, you'll find it. These ID tags also give a lot of other information about where the car was made, what kind of paint it has, and so on, but you needn't worry about these. I have included a Specifications Record sheet at the end of *Auto Repair for Dummies* to provide a place to keep all this information handy. It also has room for you to list the numbers and specifications of the things you should be replacing at regular intervals. Once this sheet contains the necessary data for each of your cars, you will be able to take it to the auto parts store with you and keep it handy when you are working on your car. If you don't want to take the book along, and you have reservations about tearing out pages, you might want to have it photocopied before you fill it out, so you will have copies for future use.

PART II
On the Road

You're out there on the road, feeling fine. You've taken all the necessary steps to keep your car in shape, and the car is humming happily along. Now that the car's needs are taken care of, it's time to learn a few tricks that will help you help yourself—and help the environment as well.

How to "Fill 'Er up" Yourself

Although most gas stations now offer you the chance to pay less per gallon if you pump the gas yourself, I've been surprised to find that many people still pay a higher price for service because they're too embarrassed to ask an attendant to show them how to do it, or because they think the job is dirty and difficult. Even if you're rich and lazy, it still pays to know how to pump your own gas. Many stations are self-service only, and you never know when you'll need to use one.

Here's how to pump your own gas:

1. Look at the price window on the pump. If there is a price registered there, have the attendant clear the machine so that the price window reads "$0.00."

2. Move the little handle on the pump to the "ON" position.

3. Remove the cap from your fuel tank.

4. Take the pump nozzle off the pump and place it into the fuel tank opening.

5. There is a trigger on the pump nozzle. When you press it, gasoline flows out of the hose and into your fuel tank. There is usually a little latch near the trigger which will keep the trigger open so that you don't have to stand there holding it. Don't worry about overflows; these pumps automatically stop pumping gasoline when your tank is almost full.

6. When the gasoline stops flowing (you'll know because those numbers in the window of the pump will stop moving), remove the pump nozzle from your fuel tank. If you want to bring the price up to an even figure, you can add a small additional amount of gasoline by pressing the trigger on the pump nozzle and watching the figures on the pump. I don't do this, because I don't want to overfill my tank—if the gasoline is right up to the top of the tank, it might leak out. Another reason for not "topping off" your tank is that if you fill up when the car is cold and then park in the sun, the gas will expand and run out through an overflow outlet, causing waste, pollution, and a fire hazard.

7. Return the pump nozzle to the pump. Find the attendant who will then write the bill for the amount shown on the pump. *Don't* clear the pump, or you will find yourself unable to prove how much gasoline you've taken, and that could lead to a very unhappy station-attendant/customer relationship!

While you are standing around waiting for the fuel tank to fill up, you can divert yourself in a variety of ways. You can get a couple of those treated towels and some water and wash your windshield. Or you could whip out your tire gauge and check your tires and maybe add some air. Most pump areas have water faucets, towels, and air hoses near them.

Filling 'Er Up Eco-logically

Did you know that, like everything else, gasoline expands with heat? Ten gallons of gas will expand by 8/10 of a quart (that's the same as 4/5—as in a bottle of whiskey) with a temperature increase of 30 degrees. So if the day is going to be a scorcher, try to fill up in the early morning or in the evening, when the air is cooler. This way, your gas tank will hold more gasoline at no extra cost, and you won't have to make as many trips to the filling station.

If you really want to fill the tank efficiently, shake the car a bit while it is filling, to get rid of trapped air in the tank. If you think this is compulsive, consider that gas expands 1/10 of 1 percent for every 10 degrees of heat. If you are judging your fuel consumption by dividing the number of gallons in your tank into the number of miles you drove before it needed refilling, you will get more impressive results if the tank is *really* full to begin with—and not partially full of heat-expanded gasoline and partially full of air.

This does *not* mean that you should jam those extra ounces of gasoline into the tank after the filler hose has automatically shut itself off. Many station attendants like to do this because it means extra money for that extra gas, but it also increases the danger that the overfilled tank will simply run over and spill that gasoline on the ground if you should travel up a hill soon afterward or park in the heat of the sun. The lost gasoline is not only a waste of fuel, but the fumes from it contribute substantially to air pollution. So fill your tank efficiently, but don't overfill it. And check your fuel tank cap to be sure its gasket is in good shape.

How to Drive Eco-logically

In the past few years, concern for the environment has ceased to be confined to members of the Sierra Club and "little old ladies with shopping bags" and finally become part of the popular culture. All over the country people are diligently recycling, conserving water, and screaming for restrictions on air pollution and the dumping of toxic wastes. Unfortunately, many of those same people are needlessly polluting the air and dumping toxic chemicals. Every gallon of gasoline they use creates toxic exhaust fumes, and they are wasting gas every time they take the car on the road.

There is a direct relationship between good mainten-ance and fuel economy: if your car is well tuned and lubricated, its mileage will improve; but there are ways to drive more efficiently and streamline a car that can have even greater effects on the amount of gas it needs to get from here to there. So here are some ways to do your bit for the ecology when you and your car are on the road. I call it "eco-logic" because it makes sense to view your car and your driving techniques from an environmental perspective as well as from an automotive point of view. The two are intimately related, as you will see.

Starting Up Without Warming Up

When you start your car in the morning, do you warm it up before you drive off? No good! Most manuals will caution you not to indulge in lengthy warm-ups. They waste fuel, pollute the air, and increase wear on your car.

You not only waste fuel by sitting there with the engine idling at *zero* miles to the gallon, if you happen to be sitting in a closed garage you can waste *yourself* with carbon monoxide fumes. If your car keeps stalling unless you warm it up and your car has a carburetor, see pages 74–75 for instructions on how to check and adjust the choke.

If your carburetor is properly adjusted and the car still doesn't seem to warm up properly until you've driven it for several miles, it might be the thermostat that's at fault. The thermostat keeps the water from circulating out of the engine until the engine warms up. This helps the engine to warm up more quickly. If your thermostat is on the blink, the whole process will take longer. Consult Chapter 8 of

Auto Repair for Dummies for instructions on locating, testing, and replacing your thermostat.

Checking Your Car Out Eco-logically

While you're at it, take a look at your air cleaner. If the air filter is dirty, you can lose a mile per gallon at 50 mph. Remember, if you can improve your mileage by only 10 percent, you can save an average of 77 gallons a year! According to the Automotive Parts and Accessories Association (APAA), if every car owner saved just one gallon a week, the nation could save more than 300,000 barrels of fuel per year!

Other things to check:

The PCV Valve

If your PCV valve is not functioning properly, you are going to be running your engine less efficiently, and you might be burning and polluting your oil, too. Check it according to the instructions in Chapter 7 of *Dummies*.

The Spark Plugs

Misfiring spark plugs can cost you up to 25 percent in mileage! If your ignition system is overdue for a tune-up, do it—or have it done—now! A simple tune-up can reduce carbon monoxide and hydrocarbon exhaust emissions (that's air pollution, folks) by 30 to 50 percent! It is also a good idea to examine at least one spark plug every 5,000 miles, to be sure your car is running efficiently. If you check at least one of your plugs against the chart in Chapter 5 of *Dummies*, it will tell you if you are running too hot, burning oil, or losing power in some other manner.

The Fan Belt and Other Drive Belts

Since these belts connect your fan, water pump, alternator, and a variety of other devices, a belt that's too loose or too tight can result in a serious loss of efficiency. It should have about half an inch of "give" and should not be frayed or badly worn. A properly adjusted fan belt will keep your battery charged and help you to start faster, with less fuel consumption. Part I of this book tells you how to check and adjust a fan belt.

OK. Now you are ready to get in and drive away.

Eco-logical Driving Techniques

First, you must view your driving techniques in terms of *fuel consumption*. In other words, if you are driving at 55 mph and you accelerate to 65 mph and have to step on the brake after a block or two, you have wasted the gasoline it took to accelerate the car, because you've had to return to the original speed so soon. So check before putting on extra speed to be sure you won't have to waste that effort by slowing for a blinker, crossroad, or curve ahead. This kind of thinking is the key to driving efficiently. Every time you step on the gas pedal you are using gas. Every time you step on the brake pedal you are losing the speed that you used the gas to achieve.

Avoid Fast Starts

It takes power to move a car from a stationary position. Either you can apply that power efficiently, by starting and accelerating slowly, or you can blow the whole thing by slamming on the accelerator for a quick getaway. A fast start may cost you 8 miles per gallon for the first 4 miles. A slow start can carry you 50 percent further on the same amount of gas! Try to go slowly, at least for the first mile. Once you are underway, keep an eye on the speed limits and pace yourself accordingly, especially in city traffic. Unless you are racing the stork to the hospital, you will probably want to keep within the speed limits anyway. So if the limit on a city street is 35 mph, don't jump off at each light, speed down the street, and have to stop for the light at the end of each block. Those traffic lights are set for the speed limit. If you maintain a nice, steady 35, you will find that the lights will magically turn green as you approach them and you will not have to stop—or start—so often. Results: less work for you and 15 percent less fuel consumed. The AAA reports that your gasoline efficiency could be increased by as much as 44 percent if all your stop-and-go driving techniques were improved!

Stay in Lane

What about changing lanes and passing other cars on the freeway? Each time you do this you accelerate to pass or change lanes and then usually have to step on the brake to fit back into the traffic pattern. The result is up to 30 percent more fuel wasted. Try to stay in lane if you can. And when you get stuck behind a slowpoke, wait for the opportunity to pass without any automotive histrionics.

Drive Smoothly

My mother used to tell me that the mark of a fine chauffeur was that the passengers were never aware that the car was moving. She never had a chauffeur, to my knowledge, but she was—and is—a good driver. She taught me never to stop short if I could help it, but to anticipate the stop and to slow down gradually. Sometimes you can slow down by just taking your foot off the accelerator. Great! You can't use extra gasoline when your foot is off the gas pedal. The same goes for dramatic changes in speed. Try to set a steady pace on the road and around the curves. If you are not speeding, you may be able to account for a lot of the slowdowns by decelerating, rather than by braking. You won't wear out your brakes as quickly, and you will save fuel. If you have a manual transmission, you can downshift to slow down, as well.

Try to accelerate slowly and smoothly. It may fool your car into not supplying an unneeded extra squirt of fuel to your engine, especially if you're going to have to slow down soon anyway.

Modern fuel-injected cars have computers that constantly measure out the minimum amount of fuel required for ever-changing road conditions, but unless you drive eco-logically, a lot of this "edge" will be lost.

Be a "Feather Foot"

Arrange your car seat so that you are as comfortable as possible. Research has shown that a comfortable driving position will help you to tread lightly on the gas pedal. A light foot on the gas pedal saves gas. By traveling at 50 mph, a "featherfoot" can get 20 percent better gas mileage than someone can who is tromping on the pedal and doing 70. This is because wind resistance increases at higher speeds, and every mile per hour over 50 costs you more than 1 percent, and so on. Besides, your car's chassis will age twice as fast at 70 mph! It may get you there sooner, but will it be waiting for you when you're ready to go home?

Drive Like A "Pro"

When you approach a hill, try to build up speed slowly before you get there. The extra momentum will carry you at least part of the way up the hill. Don't accelerate to maintain your speed while you are climbing unless you are holding up traffic. Try to keep the gas pedal steady, and never, never crest the top of a hill at high speeds; you'll only have to brake on the way down, wasting the gas that got you up there so quickly in the first place. Try coasting down the other side, using the weight of the car and its momentum to carry you down with your foot off the accelerator.

Use the Transmission

You can use your transmission to save fuel, too. If you have an automatic transmission, ease up on the gas pedal at around 18 to 22 miles an hour. This will allow the transmission to shift into high gear more easily. As you may remember, the higher the gear, the less strain on the engine—and the less fuel consumed. Does the car have overdrive? It can save another 10 percent! Owners of cars with manual transmissions can do the same thing by shifting into higher gears as soon as possible. The APAA suggests that you shift into second gear at about 5 to 8 miles per hour and into higher gears at the lowest speed that the engine will take without laboring or lugging. If you haven't already practiced this, start now.

Avoid Left Turns

Here's a really way-out way to save gas. Did you know that a *left turn* uses more gas than a right turn? That's because you generally have to wait, with the car idling at 0 mph, until the road is clear for the turn. Then you have to overcome inertia and get into low gear to get moving again. If you really want to be a gas saver, try to structure your trips around the city to include as few left turns as possible. By the same thinking, it is more eco-logical to go around the block than to make a U-turn if the turn involves a lot of stopping and starting as you shift from forward to reverse, and to forward again. A nice slow cruise around the block uses less gasoline and probably won't take much more of your time.

Structure Your Trips

While you are tinkering around with structuring trips to save gas, try the following:

1. Don't make a lot of little trips; keep a list and combine them into one longer one. A one-mile trip on a cold engine can cut fuel economy by as much as 70 percent.

2. Eliminate unnecessary trips by letting your fingers do the driving through the phone book, or by writing letters.

3. Arrange a car pool to work or to school if you can. These are not only eco-logical; they often result in new friendships as well.

4. Have you ridden a bike lately? How about the bus?

5. A local store may have slightly higher prices than the one at the edge of town, but in terms of time, gasoline, and

wear and tear on your car, the neighborhood store may be cheaper. If you are committed to the distant markets, experiment with shopping only once a week or every ten days, instead of hopping over there whenever you run out of something. You can car-pool to those distant shopping centers, too.

6. If you can, choose your routes carefully. A "short-cut" over a poorly paved road can cost 15 percent in fuel penalties—and a gravel road ups that figure to 35 percent!

Streamlining Your Car Eco-logically

We've already mentioned *wind resistance* and its relation to mileage. Take a tip from racing drivers and from the designers of fast cars and planes. Look at your car to see what you can do to cut down on wind resistance and otherwise improve its fuel consumption:

Roof Racks and Bumper Racks

Those light-looking *roof racks* are deceptive. They create quite a bit of drag, especially when fully loaded, and the ensuing wind resistance substantially interferes with the air flow around the car. As a matter of fact, a small trailer loaded with the same gear is probably not as big a liability. Trailers travel in the "wake" of the car and meet with less air resistance. Of course they weigh more too, but once underway, they follow along easily if you don't try to speed. Besides, you always disconnect the trailer when you don't need it, but you tend to carry the empty roof rack around even when you have no load to put on it.

Make sure that the bindings which hold the racks in place are secure, and be sure that everything is tied down and covered so that it can't shift or be blown away.

Inspect all the straps, rubber parts, and other gadgets involved with the racks periodically to be sure they aren't deteriorating from age, wind, sun, etc.

Be sure that front- or rear-bumper bike or ski racks don't obstruct visibility. They should not interfere with access to the trunk or the hood, but if this is unavoidable, be sure you know how to remove them easily in case of emergency.

Windows vs. Air Conditioning

Open side windows also increase wind resistance. Try to use the interior vents and the vent windows whenever you can. An *air-conditioner* may seem to be a good answer in terms of wind resistance, but you will still lose mileage if you have one. First, the car has to carry around the weight of the air-conditioner and its coolant. Second, it has to put out extra power to make the air-conditioner work. You pay your money and you take your choice—air-conditioners consume an extra 2½ miles per gallon!

Tires

Did you know that *radial tires* can save you up to 10 percent in fuel consumption? They roll more freely than conventional tires do. If you car cannot use—or does not need—radial tires, you can compromise with bias-belted tires the next time you need tires.

Underinflated tires consume about 1 mile per gallon of extra gasoline. And they wear out faster, too. Air costs nothing, so be sure your tires are getting all they need. On long trips, add about 4 pounds more than is recommended to your tires, but don't go above 32 psi. To get an accurate reading, always put air into your tires in the morning before you drive the car (except to get to the air pump, of course). After a car has been driven for a while, the tires heat up and the air in them expands. Get the snow tires off the car as soon as possible—they consume a lot more fuel, too.

Check Brakes

Check your *brakes* if you haven't already done so. Sometimes a poorly adjusted brake will "drag" while the car is in motion. It takes more power to move the wheel against the dragging brake, and the result is that your brake linings—and the gas in your tank—won't last as long. To check for dragging brakes, jack up each wheel and spin it. If a brake shoe is dragging, you will feel it as you try to turn the wheel on the hub.

Check Wheel Bearings

Worn wheel bearings will cut fuel mileage in the same way. Check them at the same time by listening for a rumbling sound as you spin each wheel. If your bearings or your brake shoes seem to be preventing your wheels from moving freely, have the situation remedied quickly or you will soon be paying for new brake linings, a new brake drum, or a worn axle.

Weight

The overall *weight* of your car is significant, too. Every 500 pounds of chrome, steel, and power accessories which you haul around will cost you from 2 to 5 miles per gallon! A car that weighs only 2,500 pounds can get you twice the mileage of a car that weighs 5,000 pounds. And it will get you there just as fast . . .

Clean Trunk Compartment

While you are at it, clean the junk out of the *trunk compartment*. You use extra fuel to haul that weight around, too.

Buy Compact Cars

Possibly the most dramatic way to save fuel is to trade that faithful old gas-eater in for a good used *compact car*. Most small cars don't need power accessories either, so you win twice. And while you are considering it, did you know that a car with a big, wide front-end creates enough wind resistance to substantially increase its fuel consumption over that of a car with a smaller, narrower front-end?

Rear Axle Ratio

How about this one for eco-logical sophistication: A car with a 10-percent-higher *rear axle ratio* can save you from 2 to 4 percent in mileage. It really doesn't matter if you don't know what rear axle ratio is; just look at the specs the next time you are trying to choose another car and pick the one with the higher ratio if everything else is equal. The higher the rear axle ratio, the slower the engine has to turn at any given speed. That's why it saves you fuel.

Wash and Wax Your Car

This is not to impress the public! A highly waxed surface improves the air flow and will decrease your fuel consumption. It will also make it easier to remove dead bugs and dirt after the trip. For instructions, see Chapter 16 of *Dummies*.

Travel Light

When packing your gear for a trip, view the entire car as a backpack. This is not a joke. It takes a great deal of energy to tote a heavy pack around, and carrying extra weight in the car will consume energy, too—the kind you pay for at a gas station. So, weigh each decision carefully when packing for the trip. Follow the old camping adage: *When in doubt, leave it out!* Remember, the less you tote along, the less you will have to pack and unpack, as well.

Symptoms of Trouble Ahead

As you drive your car, try to become more sensitive to its signals. Paying swift attention to something that sounds or smells "funny" or just doesn't feel "right" can help you catch potential trouble before it develops into a dangerous or expensive condition. Following are some "funny" things to be aware of.

Sounds

✸ *If a fan belt (or any other belt) is singing,* readjust or replace it. It should have at least half an inch of play in it and shouldn't be frayed, cracked, or glazed on the underside. Some belts tend to sing more than others. Rubbing a bit of petroleum jelly on the V-shaped undersides of these usually quiets them down. Don't drive with a broken fan belt. If you carry a spare or an old belt in the car, you may be able to save yourself towing charges.

✸ *If your radiator is singing,* check the cap. The rubber gasket may be worn and steam from the hot engine may be escaping past it.

✸ *If your tires are squealing on curves,* and you aren't speeding, check treads and alignment.

● *If your tires are "tramping,"* check inflation, tire wear, and wheel balance.

● *If something is ticking rhythmically while your engine is idling,* shut off the engine, wait ten minutes and then check the oil level. The hydraulic lifters that operate your valves can make these noises if you are down as little as a quart of oil. If the level is low, add oil up to the "full" line on the dipstick and check again in a couple of days. If you have enough oil, have a mechanic check the valve adjustment if your car has adjustable valves—some do not. Faulty valves can seriously affect your car's performance and fuel consumption.

● *If there's a knocking sound in your engine,* stop the car and call for road service. It may just be a loose rocker arm, but if it's a loose bearing or a faulty piston, it can destroy the whole engine if you let it go unheeded.

● *If there's a whistling noise* coming from under the hood, check the hoses for vacuum leaks. If it's inside the car, patch the weatherstripping according to the directions in Chapter 17 of *Dummies*.

● *If there's an unlocatable sound,* get an old stethoscope from a medical supply house or ask the family doctor. Take off the rubber disc and insert a piece of tubing in its place (about 1½ inches will do). Then put the plugs in your ears, run the engine, and move the tube end of the stethoscope around the hood area. It will amplify the

wrench will work this way too. Place one end of the wrench on the bone behind your ear, and, leaning over, place the other end of the wrench on the parts that seem to be the source of the noise. Be careful not to get a shock or get your hair tangled in the fan.

Small
tube

A Piece of Tubing and an
Old Stethoscope Make an Efficient
Trouble-Shooting Device

⚙ *If your brakes are squealing,* the brake linings may be greasy, glazed, or worn. Some disc brake pads have built-in wear sensors that squeal when it's time to replace them. Even though some disc brakes tend to squeal under normal circumstances, it's safer to have the brakes checked, or follow the instructions in Chapter 10 of *Dummies* and check them yourself.

⚙ *If the car sounds like an old taxi,* especially when it is driven on a bumpy road, it probably just needs lubrication. You may get used to the squeaks and groans, but they also indicate wear, because they are caused by parts rubbing together or moving without the proper lubrication.

⚙ *If the car is idling with an offbeat rhythm,* it is not becoming creative, it is probably misfiring; one of the spark plugs or one of the cables that connect them to the distributor cap may be at fault. An easy way to see whether or not your car is idling evenly is to place your hand, or a stiff piece of paper, against the end of the tail pipe while the car is idling (with the emergency brake on, please). Either will amplify the sound and enable you to hear the rhythm. A misfiring cylinder will come through as a pumping or puffing sound.

    a. *With the engine off,* check the spark plug cables for breaks or shorts in the wiring.

    b. *With the engine off,* remove the spark plugs one at a time and check to see if they're clean

and properly gapped. Replace any that are
fouled or burned.

c. If that doesn't help, have a mechanic check
the ignition system with an engine analyzer.
People used to check spark plugs by holding
them close to a metal surface to see whether
a spark jumped across when the engine was
cranked, but the high voltage in most ignition systems now makes that procedure extremely dangerous.

● *If the idling is rough but even,* the carburetor may need
to be adjusted. Chapter 7 of *Dummies* shows how to do
this yourself. If that doesn't work, you may need a new
carburetor. Fuel-injected cars don't have carburetors, and
a mechanic must check and adjust these complex electronic systems. Check the compression in each cylinder,
following the instructions on pages 342–343 of *Dummies*.
If the engine needs rebuilding, you may prefer to get
another engine—or another car.

● *Engine knocks or pings.* Check your timing; check the
octane of the fuel you are using. The owner's manual will
tell you the proper octane and whether the fuel should be
leaded, low-lead, or unleaded. Check the cooling system.
Do a compression check on the engine cylinders.

● *Engine misses while idling.* Check the points and the
idle speed screws on the carburetor, and look for leaky
vacuum hoses.

● *Engine misses at high speeds.* Check the points, spark
plugs, fuel pump, fuel filter, and carburetor.

⬤ *Engine misses or hesitates during acceleration.* Check the accelerator pump in the carburetor, the spark plugs, the distributor, and the timing.

⬤ *If your car sounds like a jet plane* or makes some other kind of really loud abnormal sound, a hole in the muffler is probably the cause. Replace it immediately: traffic cops hate noisy mufflers, and carbon monoxide hates people!

⬤ *If the horn is stuck,* your car is producing probably the worst noise it can make. Before this happens, have someone honk your horn until you can locate it under your hood. There are usually two horns. Each has a wire leading to it. If your horn gets stuck, pull these wires and it will stop. (Sometimes you have to pull only one.) When you have the horn fixed, tell the mechanic that you pulled the wires, and find out why the horn got stuck. (If you can't get at the horn wires, disconnect one battery terminal or pull the fuse that goes to the horn to stop the noise.)

⬤ *If you hear something squeaking, rattling, or vibrating,* Chapter 17 of *Dummies* tells you how to locate the sound and remedy the situation.

Smells

⬤ *Do you smell rubber burning under the hood?* One of your hoses might have come loose and landed on a hot part of the engine. Rescue it before it melts through.

⚫ *Do you smell burned rubber with the hood closed?* Feel your wheels. If one is hot, a brake shoe may be dragging or you may have left the parking brake on.

⚫ *Do you smell oil burning?* First check the dipstick; your oil gauge may be lying and you may be out of oil. Or your engine may be overheating and your temperature gauge may be broken. If neither is the case, look around the engine for an oil leak that may be frying in the heat of the running engine. If the oil situation seems to be OK, check the transmission fluid dipstick. Sometimes a faulty vacuum modulator can siphon the fluid out of the transmission and feed it to the engine, where it is burned. Also, if the transmission fluid is very low, it can be burned in the transmission because the gears are not lubricated enough and are getting very hot.

⚫ *Do you smell oil or exhaust fumes in the passenger compartment?* The cause could simply be burned oil from the engine area—but it could also be a faulty exhaust pipe under the car which is letting exhaust gases get into the car through the floorboards. Exhaust fumes are full of carbon monoxide, so if you smell oil or exhaust in the car, be sure to keep your windows open at all times and have the problem checked out as quickly as you can. We've all heard stories about people who have died on the highway from carbon monoxide or from passing out at the wheel because of it. Such stories are true.

⚫ *Do you smell gasoline?* Check your carburetor to be sure it isn't leaking fuel. If it seems all right, check down the fuel line all the way to the fuel tank for leaks. A look under the car, after it has been parked overnight, may help, but remember that fuel evaporates quickly, so the clues may be stains rather than wet spots. Check your fuel pump for fuel leaks. The gasoline will wash a clean streak across it, which can be seen with the naked eye.

Strange Sensations

This is a catchall category for those things that just "feel funny." Use the process of elimination to check anything that may cause your car to run roughly: hoses, tires, brakes, oil levels, and spark plug connections; the carburetor, cooling system, clutch, gear-shift, and steering linkage. If steering is difficult and you have power steering, check the dipstick in the reservoir attached to the power-steering unit to see if there's enough power-steering fluid in it. If it's low again soon after you've filled it, check for leaks in the hoses leading from the unit to the front wheels.

Incidentally, if your car has been hesitating when you change gears, the first thing to check is the transmission fluid level before you let anyone start talking about "bands." If you are burning white smoke from under your car, you probably need transmission fluid badly, although it can also be a bad vacuum modulator. If the smoking has been going on for a long time, you may need a new transmission!

Smoke Signals

If there is smoke coming out of the tail pipe, check for one of these:

● *If it is a cold morning,* you may see some white water vapor. Disregard it if it stops when the car warms up.

● *If white vapor continues to come out of the tail pipe* after the car is warm, a cracked engine block or cylinder head may be letting water leak into the engine.

● *If black smoke comes out of the tail pipe,* you may need only to adjust the carburetor because the fuel/air mixture is too rich. You can check this by running your finger around the inside edge of the tail pipe (make sure first that it is not hot). If carbon comes off on your finger, the mixture is probably too rich. Ask your mechanic to adjust it if you take the car in for a checkup.

● *If there is light or dark-blue smoke coming out of the tail pipe,* your car is burning oil. This can indicate that the car needs its piston rings replaced because oil is leaking into the combustion chambers.

● *If the smoke is light gray,* the car may be burning transmission fluid. Check the transmission dipstick. Is the fluid dark and burned-looking, or does it smell? Have the transmission checked by your mechanic. Sometimes a faulty vacuum modulator can suck transmission fluid into the engine, where it is burned in the cylinders, causing the same type of smoke to come out of the tail pipe. If this is the case, you can usually replace the vacuum modulator yourself quite easily. All you usually have to do is unscrew the old one and screw in the new one.

Preventive Medicine

Two things should have emerged as a result of all the above. The first is that most of the things that go wrong with your car can be avoided by simply maintaining it properly—lubricating it frequently and replacing fan belts, wiring, hoses, points, plugs, brake linings, and other parts *before they fail*. It is much simpler to diagnose car failure if you know that you've checked certain parts and systems recently and that they are in good shape. This is preventive medicine, and it is well worth the effort!

The second is that by understanding the way your car works, by exploring a failure logically in terms of what is happening (or not happening) and which part or parts are involved in that function, and by checking them to see if they are working properly, you will be able to quickly diagnose—and sometimes remedy—the situation. You won't feel helpless or bewildered, perhaps just frustrated by the time it sometimes takes to fix the trouble. And once you become familiar with the way things *should be*, and know why, you will be much more alert to the signs of disaster *before* disaster strikes.

PART III

Dealing with the Unexpected

One of the most exciting things about this world is the fact that, no matter how wise or well prepared you are, the unexpected is sure to occur. Some people call it The Cosmic Joke and take responsibility for their mishaps; others blame "bad luck," the government, or their mates. One thing is certain: whether you see yourself as "creator" or "victim," it's how you react to these surprises that really makes the difference. Here's how to deal with the most common bumps and trials you may meet along the way:

What to Do if Your Car Won't Start

Some fine day, when you're late for work or the dentist, you'll bounce happily out of the house and into the car and it will sit there smugly and refuse to start. After you've finished banging your head on the steering wheel, here's what to do to get Old Faithful moving again:

If you have left your lights, heater, radio or some other electrical gizmo on after you parked the car, then you know what the trouble is. Your battery is dead. You can use jumper cables to get going again if you know how to jump a start from some Good Samaritan's car, with an important exception: If either car has electronic systems, the use of jumper cables *may* damage it. If your car is one that may be damaged in this way, there may be a warning to that effect in the owner's manual or on a decal under the hood. To be sure, ask your dealer. Here's the safest way to jump-start your car:

How to Jump a Start

1. If you have found a Good Samaritan, be sure his or her battery has at least as much voltage as your own. It doesn't matter if your car has a negative ground and the GS's car has a positive ground, or if your car has an alternator and the GS's car has a generator, as long as you hook up the cables properly (and the proper way is the same in every case).

2. Take out those nice jumper cables you bought as soon as you read about them in Part I. If you didn't, you'll have to find a Good Samaritan who has cables too.

3. Place both cars in "Park"—or "Neutral" for cars with manual transmissions—with ignitions shut off and emergency brakes on. Remove the caps from both batteries (unless they're sealed) because batteries produce explosive hydrogen gas, and a spark could set it off. If the caps are open, you can avoid such an explosion.

4. The positive cable has red clips at either end, and the negative cable has black clips. First, attach one of the red

clips to the positive terminal of your battery (it will have "pos" or "+" on it, or it will be bigger than the negative terminal). Then attach a red clip to the positive terminal of the GS's car.

5. Now attach one of the black clips to the negative terminal on the GS's battery and the last black clip to an unpainted metal surface on your car that isn't near the carburetor or battery and isn't aluminum.

Connect the Positive Cable to Each Battery
and Then the Negative Cable

6. Get into your car and try to start it. If it won't, check to be sure the cables are properly connected. If they are, your battery may be beyond help, but have the GS run his or her car for 5 minutes with the jumper cables connected, and try to start your car again.

7. Disconnect the cables, thank the Good Samaritan, and resume your life.

If your alternator light stays on, or your gauge continues to point to "Discharge" after your car's been running, check your fan belt to see that it is tight enough to run your alternator properly. If your battery keeps going dead, have it and your alternator checked professionally. In any case, do not drive around with a light or gauge that reads "Trouble"; have it checked out immediately—that's why they put those gauges in there.

Other Symptoms to Look For

Here are some other common reasons why your car might refuse to start. If you encounter problems in locating parts or need more detailed information in order to make repairs, *Auto Repair for Dummies* will show you what to do:

⚙ *Car is silent when key is turned in ignition.* Check battery terminal cable connections. If they look very corroded, force the point of a screwdriver (with an insulated or wooden handle) between the connector and the post and twist it to lodge it firmly. Then have someone try to start the car. If it starts, you need to clean or replace your cables.

⚙ *Car makes a clicking noise but won't start.* Usually a dead battery. If not, check the starter wiring for a loose connection.

⚙ *Car won't start on cold mornings.* Check the choke.

Remove the air cleaner (the large pot that holds the air filter) and look down the carburetor barrel. Looking up at you is the choke, which consists of a little butterfly valve that can open and close, and a means of adjusting it. When the car is cold, the butterfly valve should remain closed to help you get the car started and warmed up faster. Is the valve closed? If not, step on the gas pedal a couple of times. It should close. Once the car is warmed up, it should open again. *Don't let anyone step on the accelerator pedal while you are looking down the carburetor.* It could backfire.

If you are driving a car with a manual choke (there are still a couple of these venerable oldtimers on the road), push the knob on the dashboard in and out to see whether the choke opens and closes.

When You Look Down the Carburetor Barrel,
You Can See the Choke Butterfly

If the butterfly valve refuses to move, it may simply be stuck because of poor lubrication or dirt. Try wiggling it with your finger. If that doesn't work, squirt a little spray lubricant on the moving parts. If this doesn't work, see Chapter 7 of *Dummies* for instructions on how to adjust the choke.

💥 *Car starts but dies or doesn't warm up for several miles.* If your choke appears to be working properly but the car continues to stall, your idle speed may be too low. Chapter 7 of *Dummies* can show you how to adjust it but you'll need a mechanic if your car is fuel-injected.

💥 *Car cranks over but won't start.* Check your distributor cap according to the instructions on page 91. If that's not your problem, check the fuel supply to your carburetor according to the instructions on pages 96–97. (If your car is fuel-injected, you won't be able to do this.)

💥 *Car won't start on rainy days.* Remove the distributor cap and check inside it for dampness. If you find moisture, squirt some mechanic's solvent into the cap, swish it around and pour it out. Then dry the cap thoroughly and replace it. The solvent will evaporate the water. Do *not* use gasoline; a spark can ignite the fumes.

💥 *Car is out of gas.* You may think, "If I got home there must be some fuel in the tank," but I've known several faithful cars that managed to limp home on a tank so empty that there wasn't enough fuel to crank them up in the morning. As a last resort, try adding gasoline to the tank no matter what the gauge on the dashboard says. They've been known to lie, you know . . .

How to Change a Flat Tire

Even if you are a member of the AAA, there is always a chance that you will find yourself stuck with a flat tire on a remote road with no telephone in sight. On these occasions, all traffic generally vanishes, leaving you helpless unless you know how to do the job yourself. We all have a general idea of what's involved, but there are a couple of places where the job gets sticky, and unless you are properly equipped, you can find yourself out of luck and in for a long wait for help to come along.

Remove the hub cap and loosen the lug nuts *before* you jack up the car. Once the car is jacked up, the wheel will turn freely, and it will be harder to get the hub cap off and almost impossible to start the nuts.

How to Remove a Hub Cap

1. Use a screwdriver or the flat end of a lug wrench to pry the hub cap off. Just insert the point where the edge of the cap meets the wheel and apply a little leverage. The cap should pop off. You may have to do this in a couple of places; it's like prying a nonscrew cap off a jar of jelly.

2. Lay the cap on its back so you can put the lug nuts into it to keep them from rolling away and heading for the nearest sewer.

You Can Use a Screwdriver to
Pry a Hub Cap Loose

How to Loosen Lug Nuts

1. These are those big nuts under the hub cap that hold the wheel in place. They are usually retightened with a power tool by most garages, and unless you've done the job yourself by hand, they are going to be pretty hard to get started. If you've taken my earlier advice and bought a cross-shift lug wrench, now is the time to pat yourself on the back. Before you begin, you will have to ascertain

whether the lug nuts on the wheel you are working on are right-hand threaded or left-hand threaded. This is not a "left-handed hammer joke"; the threads determine which way you have to turn the wrench. The lug nuts on the right side of a car are always right-hand threaded, but the nuts on the left side *may* be left-hand threaded. Look at the lug nuts on your car. In the center of the lugs you will either see an "R" or an "L" or no letter at all. Lugs with an "R," or with no letter, are right-threaded. Lugs with an "L" are left-threaded. You turn right-threaded nuts *counter-clockwise* to loosen them. You turn left-threaded nuts *clockwise*. Frankly, the whole thing seems crazy to me, but that's how it is, friends. For the purposes of sanity, let's assume that your car has right-threaded nuts. If you have a couple of lefties, just use the wrench in the opposite direction, OK?

2. Find the end of the wrench that fits the lug nuts on your car and fit it onto the first nut. Always work on lug nuts in rotation. That way you won't forget to tighten any later. Apply all your weight to the bar on the *left*. This should start the nut turning *counterclockwise*, which will loosen it. If the nut has been put on with a power tool and you can't get it started, a piece of hollow pipe, fitted over that left-hand arm of the cross-shaft wrench, will magically add enough leverage to start the nut easily. After you've replaced the nut yourself, this aid will no longer be necessary. But remember, the longer the arms on your lug wrench, the more leverage it will give you.

A Hollow Pipe and a Cross-Shaft Wrench
Can Loosen the Tightest Lug Nuts

3. Do not remove the lug nuts completely; just get them loose enough so you can remove them by hand once the car has been raised. Now you're ready to jack up the car.

How to Jack Up Your Car

1. Check your owner's manual for the proper place to position the jack for your car. If you have no manual, follow these guidelines:

Never place the jack so that the weight of the car rests on something that can bend, break, or "give." Try to place the jack so that it will touch either the car frame or the big bar that supports the front wheel suspension. Jacks can also be placed near the rear wheel axle.

2. *The following is important!* Before you attempt to jack up your car, observe these safety precautions:

   a. *Always park the car on level ground before you jack it up.* If you get a flat tire on a hill and can't coast to the bottom without killing the tire completely, then park it close to the curb, turn the wheels toward the curb, and block the downside wheels securely to prevent the car from rolling. Even with these precautions, however, I'd be nervous.

   b. *Never jack up a car without blocking the wheels.* Even if the car is on level ground, use bricks, wooden wedges, or metal wheel chocks to block the wheels at the opposite end of the car from the end that is to be raised. This will keep the car from rolling after it has been jacked up. Keep the blocks in the trunk of your car so you won't have to go hunting around if you have to change a tire on the freeway. If you find yourself faced with the job of changing a tire and you have been foolish enough to disregard all these italics and have nothing with which to block the wheels, then at least park it near the curb with the wheels turned in. This may not keep you from getting hurt if the car rolls off the jack, but at least innocent motorists and pedestrians will not have to deal with a runaway driverless car!

c. *Be sure your car is in "Park" and that the emergency brake is on*, before you jack it up.

d. *Remove the spare from the trunk.* It's easier to do this before you jack the car up in the air. If you haven't checked your spare recently, keep your fingers crossed that there's enough air in it! Roll the spare to the scene of the action.

3. Now use the jack to raise the car. Apply nice even strokes, taking the jack handle from its lowest to its highest point on each stroke, to cut down on the labor involved. When the car is high enough so that the wheel is completely clear of the ground and you can easily reach and see whatever part concerns you, you can stop. Then, do the following:

4. If you carry jack stands, place them under the car, near the place where the jack is touching the car. Raise the stands until they are high enough to just fit under, and lock them in place. Lower the jack until the car is resting on the jack stands. Then remove the jack.

5. Before you begin to work, wiggle the car a little to make sure it is resting securely on the jack or the jack stands. This will also tell you if you have the wheels blocked properly. It is better if the car falls while all four

wheels are in place (it will just bounce a little). If you remove a wheel and begin to work without checking to be sure you've jacked it and blocked it securely, it will do itself—and you—a lot of damage if it falls. This is not meant to frighten you away from jacking up your car and working on—or under—it. It should simply dramatize that a few simple precautions will remove any danger.

6. Everything secure? Fine! Then you can go ahead and remove the lug nuts and put them into the hub cap.

How to Change the Tire

1. Grasp the flat tire with both hands and pull it toward you. It is sitting on the exposed bolts that the lug nuts screwed onto. The flat should slide along the bolts until, suddenly, it clears the end of the bolts and you find yourself supporting its full weight. Tires are heavy, and you will be quite happy to lower it to the ground (if you haven't already dropped it).

2. Roll the flat along the ground to the trunk, to get it out of the way.

3. You are now going to have to lift the spare onto the lug bolts. Since tires are heavy, you may have a little trouble lifting it into place—especially if you are not accustomed to lifting heavy things.

4. After you have the spare tire in place, replace the lug nuts and tighten them by hand. Give them each a jolt with the wrench to get them firmly into place, but wait until

the car is on the ground before you really try to tighten them down.

5. Replace the jack and lift the car off the jack stands, if you've used them, and lower the car to the ground. Once the car is resting on the ground, use the lug wrench to tighten the lugs as much as you can. You don't want to twist them off the bolts or ruin the threads, but you don't want the wheel to fall off, either. Use your hollow pipe, if you are worried about tightening them sufficiently, or step on the right-hand arm of the lug wrench after the nut is tight. Remember, right-hand threaded nuts tighten in a clockwise direction, lefties go the other way.

6. Now place the hub cap against the wheel and whack it into place with the heel of your hand. Cushion your hand with a soft rag first so you won't hurt it. Don't hit the hub cap with a wrench or a hammer—you'd dent it. Whack it a couple of times, in a couple of places, to be sure it's on evenly. Even second-hand hub caps can cost as much as $50 to $100 apiece to replace. If it is too much of a hassle, or if you don't have the time to replace the hub cap, you can take it home and install it later; it is mostly ornamental and you can drive for a while without it. But *do* replace it soon because it helps keep dust and dirt out of your brakes and bearings.

7. Put the flat into the trunk, where the spare was located, and put your tools away. Don't forget to remove the wheel blocks, and *don't forget to have that flat fixed!*

Emergency Measures When You Can't Change the Tire

If you get caught in the middle of nowhere with a flat tire and are unable to change it yourself, there is a way to get rolling again without riding on the flat. If you carry an aerosol can of *inflator/sealant*, you can simply screw the nozzle of the can onto the valve stem of the flat tire and it will fill the tire with air and some sort of goo that temporarily seals the puncture. Since there is still some question about how permanent this is and its ultimate effects on your tire, use it *only* in emergencies, get to a service station as soon as possible, and ask them to try to remove the stuff before they fix the tire.

What to Do if Your Car Drops Dead on the Freeway

Whether the car has died on the freeway or in front of the house, it is always a time of unrivaled panic and stress. But an informed, well-organized approach to diagnosing your sick monster's ills will pay off by getting you moving again with a minimum loss of time, money, and composure. The problems involved are seldom serious, and you can usually solve them by keeping a cool head and following these instructions.

First, if you are on a freeway, try to get to the righthand shoulder of the road. Very often, if a car is going to do its swan song while in motion, it will give you a couple of hints first. Be alert to any sudden loss of power. Do you suddenly have to floor the accelerator to maintain speed or to keep moving at all? Have any of your warning lights gone on? It is worthwhile to stop immediately and check the cause. Is the car suddenly running roughly? Is the engine misfiring? Are there any new noises? Is the car pulling to one side? All of these are good reasons to head for the side of the road.

Safety Precautions

While the car is still going, try to coast down the shoulder until you are well away from any curves behind you. This will pay off when you are ready to get back onto the freeway, because you will be able to spot oncoming traffic before it's on your tail.

If the car has died right on the freeway and you can't get off the road, *don't do anything!* I know that it is unnerving to sit in a dead car, with traffic piling up behind you. But it is literally suicide to attempt to cross a high-speed freeway on foot. Most freeways that are heavily traveled are also heavily patrolled, and some nice highway patrol officer will be along before you know it. Once the officer is on the scene, it will be a simple matter to stop traffic long enough to push your car to the right shoulder.

Once you have reached the side of the road, take these additional safety precautions:

1. Don't work on your car from the left side, unless you will be standing well away from the right-hand lane. If you can't move the car farther off the road, climb into the area from the front or the right, if necessary, but keep away from traffic. That goes for changing left-hand tires, too.

2. If it is daylight, put on your emergency blinkers or your left-turn signal to alert oncoming traffic to the fact that your car is not moving.

3. If it is nighttime and you carry flares, place them about six feet behind the car to alert traffic. If you don't have any flares, you may carry a lantern, a large battery-operated light, or a couple of milk cartons filled with wax and a wick. If you have nothing, leave the right-hand car door open so the interior lights will go on and alert traffic.

Once you are safely off the road and ready to deal with the problem, try to view what happened in dietary terms. Your car lives on a mixture of air, fuel, and fire—as you probably remember. If it won't go, it is not getting one of these ingredients.

If your car is fuel-injected, you don't have too many options for locating the source of the trouble. It's difficult and dangerous to monkey with the fuel-injectors, and the chances are that the little computer brain that tells your car what to do has just freaked out, but you can check the things below that have nothing to do with a carburetor before you call the AAA.

Air

This is simple and probably not the problem. The car gets its air through the air cleaner. Unless the air filter is totally clogged, it should get enough air to keep it going. Of course your choke or throttle may be stuck in a closed position, and this could keep your car from breathing properly. If your car has a carburetor, remove your air cleaner and look into the carburetor barrel. Is the choke open? Move the throttle linkage with your finger (that's the arm that makes the car rev when you push it). Does it seem to be moving freely? Then that's not your problem. Check your PCV valve to be sure it's clear and functioning. Look at those hoses—have any of them become disconnected or broken? Do you hear air whistling while the car idles—if it can? One strategic hose lost can slow or stop your car. Reclamp the wanderer or tape the hole, and you'll soon be on your way. Of course if you've made a habit of checking and replacing worn hoses before disaster strikes, you have avoided this trouble completely.

Fuel

If the car will turn over but won't start running, it may not be getting any fuel. Are you out of gas? Even if your gas gauge says you still have some, the gauge may be on the blink. When did you fill the car last?

Did you lose power before the car died? Look down the carburetor again and push the accelerator pump arm. Is fuel squirting into the venturi? Then the float bowl is full.

An In-Line Fuel Filter near the Carburetor

Still, it may not be getting a fresh supply when it needs it.

Disconnect the hose that leads from the carburetor to the fuel pump. Somewhere along the line is a little metal or plastic cylinder called the fuel filter. On most cars, the fuel filter is held in place by metal clamps on either side of it, either in the fuel line or in the carburetor inlet fitting. These are called *in-line* filters. Some cars have the fuel filter inside the carburetor or the fuel pump, but it is no more difficult to get at these. They are called *integral* filters. It is important to get in the habit of changing your fuel filter every time you tune your car, especially if you tend to ride around with an almost-empty fuel tank.

The fuel filter could have jammed—especially if it hasn't been changed in ages. Place the end of the hose in a jar or plastic bag. If you don't have anything to put it in, let it hang down so the gas can run onto the ground. Don't let gasoline run out of the hose onto your clothes or all over the engine. If it's very hot, fan the area to disburse the fumes. Bump the starter and see if gasoline squirts out of the hose. If it does, then your fuel filter and fuel pump are probably all right. If nothing comes out of the hose, you probably either have a plugged fuel filter, a defective fuel pump, a broken fuel line, or you are out of gas.

If you can, try to eliminate the fuel filter as the villain by taking it out to see if gas comes out of the hose. If it does, the filter is blocked. You can try to clear it, or replace it if you carry a spare. If you have changed the filter recently, ignore this step and look under the rear end of the car to see if fuel is leaking from a broken fuel line. If you find nothing and you fail to find any other cause of trouble, tie a white rag to your door handle or antenna and wait for help, or try to get to a phone and contact a rescue unit or the AAA. With luck, help should arrive within half an hour.

Sometimes the problem is *too much* fuel. If you open your hood and find that everything is covered with gasoline, *don't try to start the car!* Gasoline is too inflammable to monkey around with. Just hoist that white flag and get some help.

If it's a very hot day and you've been on the road in stop-and-go traffic, you may have vapor lock. See the section on overheating on pages 97–98 for what to do about this.

Fire

If the fuel is entering your carburetor as it is supposed to, then you are probably having ignition trouble. As you know, the "fire" is really electric current that is stored in the battery, replaced by the alternator, amplified by the coil, and directed by the distributor to each spark plug. If something along the way goes wrong, all the air and fuel in the world will not produce combustion in the car's cylinders, and it won't go. Since the car was running before it died, it's probably not the fault of the battery, solenoid, or starter, which brings you to the distributor cap.

With the engine off, check to see if the cables that run from the distributor cap to the spark plugs are pushed down securely at each end. Check the cable that runs from the center of the cap to the coil to be sure it, too, is secure. How about the smaller wires that come out of the coil? *Please note that because many cars now have high-energy ignition systems that operate at 47,000 volts or higher, it is unsafe to pull a distributor or spark plug cable to test for a spark.* In fact, if you have an electronic ignition system, skip the rest of the checks under this heading.

If your car has a nonelectronic ignition system, you can remove the distributor cap and look at the points. Do they open and close when you bump the starter? If not, adjust them so they do and check again for spark. If there is still no spark, your points could be oxidized, or fouled by a bit of grease or oil. Bump the engine so the points are closed, and insert the tip of a screwdriver, fingernail file, matchbook cover, or feeler gauge to rub the point surfaces to eliminate the oxidation or dirt. If you *still* don't get a spark, there's still another thing to try.

It is a good idea to keep your old rotor, points, and condenser in the trunk of your car after you replace them during a tune-up. First, try replacing the rotor with the old one. If that doesn't work, replace the condenser. If that doesn't work, replace the points. Don't worry about gapping them; as long as they open and close, the car will run. I have been told that the most frequent cause of car failure is improper lubrication of the cam when the points were changed. Because of this, the little rubbing block gets worn down, and then, even when the block rests on the cam lobe, there is not enough surface to force the points apart. That's why it's important to check your dwell every 5,000 miles and replace points at every tune-up.

If you've checked everything out and the car still won't go, then you are probably going to have to wait for help. Sometimes it's your coil or part of your engine that has given out. Sometimes it's the transmission. If that's the case, you may be saying good-bye to Old Faithful. All the comfort I can offer is that *Dummies* tells you how to buy a good new or used car. Most of the time, however, you will find the cause of the trouble by checking as I've outlined above. Or you will have plenty of warning before .

the car gives up the ghost. If you have not checked and maintained your car properly, if you have ignored the warnings, the knockings, the smoke from the tail pipe, the hesitations and the stalls, well—you asked for it.

What to Do if Your Car Overheats on a Hot Day

Even the happiest, most beautifully tuned car will overheat occasionally. If you find yourself in stop-and-go traffic, on a rotten hot day, the chances are that your car's dashboard temperature indicator will rise. There are a couple of things you can do to help your car keep its cool under these circumstances:

1. At the first sign of overheating, shut off your air-conditioner and open your car windows. This will decrease the load on the engine and help it to cool off.

2. If you continue to overheat, turn on the car heater and blower. This will transfer the heat from the engine to the interior of the car. (It will do wonders for your overheated engine but very little for you!)

3. If you are stopped in traffic and the temperature gauge is rising, shift into "Neutral" and rev the engine a little to make the water pump and the fan speed up and draw more liquid and air through the radiator. The increased air and liquid circulation should help to cool things off.

4. Try not to "ride your brakes." Brake drag increases the load on the engine and makes it heat up. Lag behind a bit if traffic is crawling, and then move up when the gap between you and the car in front of you gets too wide. Try to crawl along slowly, on little more than an idle, rather than moving up quickly and braking to a stop.

5. If you think your car is about to boil over, drive to the side of the road, open the hood, and sit there until things cool off. Remember, *don't open the radiator cap* under these circumstances, and if your engine has boiled over, *don't add water* until the car is quite cool again. If you must add water when the engine is still a little warm, add the water while the engine is running in neutral gear.

How to Remove a Radiator Cap and Add Water or Coolant to Your Radiator

1. First of all, *never* remove the cap from a radiator when the engine is hot. If your car overheats on the freeway, get to the side of the road and shut off the engine. Then just sit there for 15 or 20 minutes until things cool down. You can lift the hood to help the heat escape, but leave the radiator cap alone. Since it is automotive suicide to add cold water to a hot engine (see No. 5 below), there is no need to get the cap off until the engine cools down. Keep your cool until your car regains its own!

2. When the car is cool, lift the lever on the safety cap, to allow the pressure to escape. Then turn the cap counterclockwise to remove it. It's a good idea to place a cloth

over the cap after you've raised the lever, to keep the cap from burning your hand if it is hot.

3. If you don't have a safety cap, place a cloth over the cap and turn it counterclockwise to its first stop. This will allow the pressure to escape. If you see liquid, or a great deal of steam, escaping, retighten the cap and wait for things to cool down. If not, continue to turn the cap counterclockwise to remove it.

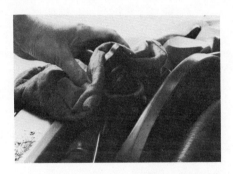

How to Remove a Radiator Cap Safely

4. When you remove the cap, *tilt* it as you remove it, so that the opening is away from you (and anyone else around). In this way, if there is still enough heat and pressure to spray hot stuff around, it will land on the engine, or inside the hood, where it can do no harm. Be particularly sure to do this if you haven't bought a safety cap.

5. *Never* add cold water to a hot engine! Adding cold water to an engine that is hot can crack the engine block, since the hot metal contracts sharply when the cold water hits it. If you must add water to an engine that is still *warm*, always do it with the engine running. This allows the cold water to join the stream of hot water that is circulating through the system, rather than falling all at once into the system when the engine is started again.

6. Add water to within a couple of inches below the cap—or to the fill line if you have one. Plain old tap water will do.

7. When you are finished, replace the cap by screwing it on, clockwise, and then push the lever down again.

Vapor Lock

I ought to say a word about a condition that may occur under overheated circumstances. This is called vapor lock, and it can be quite disconcerting if you don't know what is happening.

Occasionally a car will get so hot that the gas boils in the fuel line. When it boils, it forms bubbles that keep the fuel pump from pumping the gasoline to the carburetor. This situation is easy to spot. Your car just suddenly stops going. And the condition is easy to fix once you know what has occurred.

1. If you are on the freeway, stay in your car until a member of the highway patrol comes along and helps you

get to the side of the road. If you are in normal traffic and it is safe to get out and push the car to the side of the road, do it.

2. Once you are at the side of the road, lift the hood and place a wet cloth on the fuel line and the fuel pump. If you have no place to wet a rag, you'll just have to sit and wait until things cool off naturally. The wet rag does it much faster.

3. Once you have cooled the line until the gasoline is no longer boiling and the bubbles have dissipated, wrap the rag around the line to help keep the gasoline in the line from overheating again. (Some tinfoil wrapped around the line helps tremendously. If you often get vapor lock, carry some foil in the trunk of your car.) You can also place metal clothespins along the fuel line to radiate the heat.

4. Get back on the road as though nothing had happened. This sort of thing will occur only under extreme conditions; in most cases, if you are traveling at speeds under 25 mph or idling a lot, the fan in the car will keep the fuel cool enough to avoid vapor lock.

Other Things that Can Cause Your Car to Overheat

If your car continues to overheat you will have to look elsewhere for the cause:

Timing

If you haven't tuned and timed your car recently, it may be the fault of your timing. Late timing sometimes produces an overheated engine by having the spark fire the fuel/air mixture after the piston has moved back down from the top of its stroke. This causes the spark plugs to fire too late to allow all the gases to burn properly, and more heat will burden your cooling system. Late timing alone will not cause a car to overheat by more than a few degrees, but coupled with other problems, it can bring the temperature to a critical point. The remedy is simple: just check your timing and adjust it. Chapter 5 of *Dummies* tells you how.

Plugged Radiator

Some radiators get so plugged up with rust, sediment, or small insects that even cleaning and flushing them does not do the trick. Since plugged passages cut down on the circulation of the liquid in the system, it cannot cool efficiently. The remedy is to have the radiator removed and steam-cleaned by a radiator specialist.

Slipping Fan Belt

Check your fan belt to be sure that there is no more than about ½ inch of "give." If it is looser than that, it may not be driving your water pump properly, and that can impair circulation and overheat the cooling system. If your fan belt seems loose or very frayed, replace it according to the instructions in Chapter 5 of *Dummies*.

Collapsing Bottom Radiator Hose

Occasionally, a bottom radiator hose will begin to collapse under the vacuum created by the water pump, and the impaired circulation will cause overheating. If your car starts to overheat, stop and open the hood, with the car in "Park" and the parking brake on, without shutting off the engine. Then take a look at the bottom hose (be careful not to get your hair or clothing caught in the fan or the fan belt), and see if it has collapsed. If it has replace it.

Low Oil Level

Check your oil dipstick if you still can't find the cause of overheating. If your car is low on oil, it will tend to overheat because the oil removes from 75 to 80 percent of the "waste heat" in your engine (besides doing its other numbers). If you are one quart low in oil and your car holds 5 quarts, there is a 20-percent reduction in the amount of heat that the oil can carry away (it cools off in the crankcase).

What to Do in Case of an Accident

Nobody likes to think about the possibility of being involved in a car accident, but the fact is that they do happen occasionally, despite our best efforts to prevent them. Working on the "fire-drill principle," it's better to know what actions to take before such an emergency occurs than to be caught short in a crisis. Accordingly, let's talk about what you should do if you find yourself in such unhappy circumstances. The following guidelines should be followed, whether you are the one who caused the accident or the unfortunate victim of one:

Aiding the Injured

Obviously, anyone who is injured should command your first attention. Don't attempt to move an injured person, unless there is a danger of the car catching fire or of their getting hit by traffic. People with neck and back injuries can be more seriously injured if you move them. Although the Good Samaritan Act says you are not liable if your act is reasonable and in good conscience, you may still be sued if something you did to aid or comfort an injured person had negative effects. So unless you are qualified to administer first aid, be sure to summon help. In many communities, simply dialing 911 or the local emergency number will bring whatever aid is necessary. Coinless emergency telephones are also available along most major highways and freeways. And the highway patrol or other law-enforcement agency may monitor certain CB channels for emergency help calls.

Of course, if someone is bleeding profusely, it is of paramount importance to try to control the flow of blood rather than worrying about the legal implications. My copy of the *California Driver's Handbook* says "Bleeding: Apply direct pressure. Even severe bleeding can almost always be stopped by putting continuous pressure on the bleeding site."

If the injured person is suffering from shock, place a blanket or a coat over him to keep him warm. Aside from this, just providing love and support is probably the most effective way you can help anyone who has been hurt, unless you are trained in first aid (which isn't a bad idea, is it?).

If you injure or kill an animal, stop and try to find the owner. If you can't, call the local Humane Society and the police and stay with the animal until help arrives. If there are witnesses who can testify that you could not avoid hitting the animal, it would be wise to get their names and addresses.

Turn Off the Ignition

If any of the cars which were wrecked in the accident are still running, turn off the ignition, to avoid fires from spilled gas. No matter how shaky you are, don't smoke around the vehicles involved!

Protect Oncoming Traffic

If you can, move the vehicles out of the flow of traffic. If not, or if there is glass or oil or gasoline all over the roadway, get someone to wave approaching vehicles away from the scene, to avoid pile-ups. If you wish to use flares, be very careful not to set them anywhere near spilled gasoline! They should be placed far enough away from the accident to give oncoming traffic a chance to slow down and change lanes.

Search the Area for Victims

In a severe accident, people are sometimes thrown some distance from their vehicles. You may want to take a look around to make sure that no one is lying nearby, unobserved.

Notify the Police

In any traffic accident, you must notify the authorities. If you don't, you may have trouble recovering expenses from your insurance company and can be open to prosecution as a hit-and-run driver. Send someone to summon them, or use a roadside emergency phone, if one is available. In many states, you must fill out a written police report about even minor accidents and send a report to the state Department of Motor Vehicles as well. If you don't, you run the risk of losing your driver's license.

If you can, make a quick sketch of the accident, noting any nearby cross streets or other topography and the direction and speed of every vehicle involved and where it ended up. If there are skid marks, put them in your sketch. Don't forget the proper time and date and any unusual weather conditions that may have had a bearing on the accident.

Exchange Information

No matter how small the accident appears to be, it is important that you get the following information from the driver of each car involved and from anyone else who may have been injured:

> ▷ Name
> ▷ Address
> ▷ Phone number
> ▷ License number
> ▷ Insurance company

You will need this information in order to report the accident in the event the police don't arrive at the scene, and also for your insurance company. If you leave the scene of an accident without exchanging this information, you may be liable for legal prosecution.

Get Witnesses

All too often, drivers who have talked over a minor fender-bender at the scene and agreed that there was little or no damage, suddenly find themselves sued for "whiplash" injuries or damages to the other car—or cited for negligence, unsafe driving, or traffic violations. Therefore it is best to take whatever steps are necessary to get the details of the event down and recorded with the proper authorities right away. If there are witnesses to the accident, make every effort to get their names, addresses, and phone numbers, too. If they are uncooperative, write down the license plate numbers of their cars.

If You Are the Only Person Involved

If you hit a parked car or accidentally damage someone's property, and you can't locate the owner when the accident occurs, leave your name, address, and phone number on the car you've hit, or attached to the site of the damage. If you are driving someone else's car, leave their name and address, too. To avoid "hit-and-run" prosecution, be sure to notify the local authorities.

What to Do if You Lock Yourself Out of Your Car

Here's an "emergency" that may not be dangerous, but certainly can be exasperating! If you tend to be featherheaded and leave the keys in your car fairly often, you may be tempted to hide an extra key somewhere on your car. However, I must warn you that unless you are very clever about where you hide it, you may be inviting someone to steal your car or its contents. Those little magnetic boxes that stick to the metal surface of the body or frame are the best bets here, but be sure to place it in an obscure and hard-to-reach area where it will not jiggle loose and fall out. I leave the choice of area up to you—if I publish a list of suggestions, then the Car Thieves of America will have me up for their annual "Helpful Dummy Award"! Be imaginative. It is better to have to struggle a little to reach that extra key than to give the car away easily. And don't hide your house key with it. You don't want to give *everything* away, do you?

Assuming that you have decided not to risk hiding that extra set, here's how to get into your car without a key:

If you have conventional door locks on the car, obtain a wire coat hanger, straighten it out, bend the end of it into a little hook, and insert it between the rubber molding and the window or vent window. Then, carefully, with the dexterity of a jewel thief, hook it around the door button and pull it up.

If you or your auto manufacturer has had the foresight to replace these buttons with the new, smooth, cylindrical ones, your car has less of a chance of being stolen, and you have a harder job getting into it without a key. You might be able to hook the door handle, but most of them will straighten out your hanger before they condescend to budge.

If you call a locksmith, you will have to prove that you own the car before any work will be done, and you will probably also have to pay immediately. So let's hope that you didn't lock your wallet in there, along with your keys. If your key has been lost outside your car and your steering wheel locks, they may have to dismount the steering wheel and remove the lock—and this will cost you lots of money, time, and aggravation, before you can drive off again. However, there is good news! Each car key is coded by the manufacturer and, if you have the key code number, a locksmith can make you a new key as long as you have identification and can describe the car in terms of its vital statistics. GM car keys have little coded tags you knock out of the key and keep; other U.S. cars come with little metal tags with the number on them, and most foreign car makers engrave the number right on the keys. As a valuable favor to yourself, write down the code number where someone at home can read it to you in an emergency, and also record it, without identifying what it is, in your pocket address book or in your wallet *before you lose your keys*. If you don't know the code number of your keys, and you bought the car, new or used, from a dealer, they may still have the number on file. Failing that, a good locksmith may be able to analyze a key in fairly new condition and come up with the proper code for it. This kind of preventive work is worth doing right away, before you get into trouble!

If you should happen to lock yourself out of the car while you have the trunk open, it is sometimes possible to move the rear seat out of the way and gain access to the rear of the car, or you can hide an extra ignition key in the trunk.

If you get totally freaked out and decide to break a window, break the little vent window, if you have one. It's cheaper to replace, and sometimes the latch will break before the glass does. If you have to break the glass, wrap something around your hand and use a stone or a heavy object. Keep your head away from flying glass, although most auto glass should be shatterproof. Don't break a window that will interfere with visibility when you are driving home to face the jeers of your family and friends.

About the Author

Deanna Sclar never even *drove* a car until she was 25. Then she found herself on the California freeways, terrified her car would break down because of her ignorance. Intoxicated by the discovery that cars could be maintained with relatively little knowledge and a total lack of manual dexterity, she wrote *Auto Repair for Dummies*.

Deanna has appeared on more than 400 radio and television shows including Good Morning America, Today, Mike Douglas, A.M. Los Angeles, and the Lifetime, CNN, FNN, and National Public Radio networks. Her video, "Auto Repair for Dummies: The Maintenance Tape" was a finalist in the National Home Video Awards. She's written, produced, directed, and co-hosted "Outrageous Women," a weekly talk show, and several specials for broadcast television. She's written monthly car-care columns for *Family Circle*, *Boys' Life*, and *Exploring* and articles for such national magazines as *Redbook* and *New Woman*.

The former "Thumbs Sclar" has restored two classic cars, a truck, and a house; sailed Polynesia, the Great Barrier Reef, and the Kingdom of Tonga; and trekked alone through Southeast Asia. *Housemates: A Practical Guide to Living with Other People*, was published while she was dismasted for six weeks in mid-Pacific. "My goal is to prove that we have control over our lives. Whether you are working on a car, or making a life-long dream come true, *it's a do-it-yourself world!*"